CITY OF
SALISBURY

EDITED BY HUGH SHORTT

FOREWORD BY

Lawrence Tanner

C.V.O.

KEEPER OF THE MUNIMENTS AT
WESTMINSTER ABBEY

PHOENIX HOUSE LTD
LONDON

Printed in Great Britain
in 12 point Monotype Poliphilus
by The Aldine Press of Letchworth for
Phoenix House Ltd, 38 William IV Street,
Charing Cross, W.C.2
First published 1957

FOREWORD

By LAWRENCE TANNER, C.V.O., F.S.A.

I COUNT IT AN honour to have been asked to write a Foreword to a book which tells so delightfully the story of one of the fairest, or, as a Wiltshireman would maintain, the fairest of English cities. It is a fascinating story which it unfolds. It is not merely that the history of Salisbury touches the history of England at several points, but that again and again in the lives of its citizens, as we see them disclosed in this book, we can trace the reactions of contemporary people to movements and events which have passed into history.

It was indeed fortunate that the great decision to remove the cathedral from its windswept, fortress-dominated hill to its present site was taken at the beginning of a century when clergy and citizens alike were animated with the one overpowering desire to raise buildings to the glory of God which should be perfect in all their parts. In the best sense, as it has been well said, such an aim 'appealed equally to religious faith and human pride'; pride in work which, whether it was seen by man or was so placed that only the swallows saw it in their flight (to use Mâle's charming phrase), was as perfect as human hands could make it. It was no less fortunate that at Salisbury there were three men who typified the spirit of the age—Bishop Poore with his driving force, Elias de Dereham with his great administrative ability, inspiring ideas, and love for noble works of art, and Nicholas de Ely, the master-mason, who was able and willing to carry out those ideas and raise a building incomparable in its beauty.

But although the cathedral must always dominate Salisbury, the foundation and development of the city itself is no less interesting, as this book shows. For here we still have in essentials and in its lay-out a medieval city, and we can study in the history of its civic administration, its merchant guilds, and in the influence of its wool trade the forces which led to the greatness of England in medieval times. And here again, in the later Middle Ages, we have in John a'Porte, John Halle, and William Webbe (from whom I am proud to be descended) three typical merchant princes who have left us in their benefactions and in their houses something to show what manner of men they were and how great was their pride in the city of their birth or of their adoption.

So we can go down the centuries, pausing for a moment to note how vividly the realities of the dreaded plague are illustrated by the heroic work of John Ivie, the Mayor of 1627, who almost alone remained at his post to cope with the situation, and how curiously illuminating were the motives which induced Mr Recorder Sherfield so misguidedly to attempt to destroy the stained-glass window which seemed to him to be both idolatrous and untrue.

When we come to the second half of the seventeenth century we can see, as Canon Smethurst has pointed out, the changes in thought, in manners, and in ways of life which were taking place. The old medieval Salisbury was receding, leaving its traces behind it, but the gradual development of modern Salisbury had begun. The story of that development as it unfolds itself is no less interesting than the story which preceded it of the struggle of the citizens to free themselves from the dominating power of the bishop. Life within the city became less turbulent and more gracious. Even the houses in which the inhabitants lived reflected the change. Some of the older houses, at any rate within the Close, were altered and given 'a new look' more in keeping with the age, and the lovely late seventeenth- and early eighteenth-century houses, which are the glory of Salisbury, were built. Those who lived in them were the leaders in the social, scientific, literary, musical, and artistic activities which were so marked a feature of Salisbury life throughout the eighteenth century and afterwards.

And so the modern city emerges and, as these pages tell, its expansion within the last century or so has been astonishing. Much that has been done is pure gain, some things inevitably must cause regret, but a city which is proud of its history and mindful of the past can go forward without fear, and welcome, even in architecture, the (not too glaring) stranger within its gates. For essentially Salisbury remains the same, and every generation must be allowed to make its own contribution to its history and its architecture, always remembering, as it has been wisely said, that 'no man can serve an institution with full fidelity of comprehension who has not fed, or fed himself, on its memories'.

I was myself brought up on those memories by both sides of my family. The Eyre family, to which my mother belonged, had been associated with the city and Close of Salisbury as Members of Parliament, Recorders, mayors of the city, and cathedral dignitaries since the sixteenth century. They formed, with the families into which they married, a kind of vast cousinhood which only passed from the Close with the death of Miss Barbara Townsend in 1939, herself a link with the past, for she once told me that she could just remember the last of the sedan chairs setting down their occupants at Mompesson House, which was her home throughout her long life. On the other side, too, there was a long connection. My father's family moved to Salisbury from north Wiltshire in the middle of the eighteenth century. There they practised the law and supplied mayors for the city for three consecutive generations. The record of the gargantuan feast which my great-great-grandfather gave as mayor in 1797 has been preserved, and both at his first house within the Close and later in the old house in Castle Street (No. 45), where the music-room he added still exists, he carried on the musical traditions which had been fostered by 'Hermes' Harris at an earlier date.

So much may, perhaps, be said to explain how it comes about that I have been honoured by being asked to write a foreword to this book. For indeed for those bred on such memories with roots which go deep into its history, Salisbury must always be a city apart; so old and yet so full of life, so perfect in its setting and so unfailing in its charm.

CONTENTS

ILLUSTRATIONS

Salisbury Cathedral, by John Constable · *Frontispiece*

The copyright of the plates is reserved as follows:

W. A. Chaplin, Pls. 38, 46; Philip Glasier, 6; Phoenix House, 36; Robert Potter, 4, 5, 7, 9, 10, 12, 13, 14, 15, 16, 17, 18, 19, 20, 21, 22, 23, 24, 25, 26, 27, 28, 29, 30, 31, 32, 33, 39, 46, 47, 49; Air Ministry (Crown Copyright reserved), photo by J. K. St Joseph (Cambridge University Collection of Aerial Photographs), 2; *Salisbury Journal*, 37, 48; Victoria and Albert Museum, Frontispiece and 1.

The following were taken by David Jones: 5, 7, 9, 10, 12, 13, 19, 22, 23, 24, 25, 27, 29, 33, 49.

FIGURES IN TEXT
Drawn by Winifred Scholfield

EDITORIAL NOTE

IN 1948 an Architectural Group was formed within the Salisbury and District Society of Arts for the purpose of increasing interest in the City of Salisbury and its neighbourhood, so that a more informed public might seek to preserve its ancient buildings and the quiet beauty of its setting. Five members of the group decided that to write a book about Salisbury was a means to this end, and each of the five has contributed a chapter. Another member, Robert Potter, undertook to compile the plates, of which we all felt there should be a generous number.

We wanted to present a diorama of Old Sarum, the city on the hill, and New Sarum, the daughter-city in the plain, with particular regard to the buildings, whether magnificent or humble, which have helped to form their character, but we had no intention of adding to the long list of guide-books, and therefore decided that *City of Salisbury* must be written in the form of a history. We have not wearied the reader with a mass of footnotes and references, but we hope that the bibliographies, both general and particular, will suffice. Intentionally, we wrote little about Salisbury Cathedral, simply because so much has been written on this incomparable subject in recent years. Yet when we had finished, we felt that the omission must be compensated, and the late F. C. Eeles, with his usual generosity and scholarship, wrote a postscript which is not a description of the cathedral or a history of its building, but an account of intangible things—its organization, its liturgy and ritual which, as the Sarum Use, have made an even greater impression than the building itself on Western Christendom. This postscript was Dr Eeles's last work.

Almost at the eleventh hour we prevailed upon Lawrence Tanner, Keeper of the Muniments at Westminster Abbey, to write the Foreword to our book. Apart from being an historian, Mr Tanner is, by descent and early upbringing, a native of Salisbury and its lifelong friend, so that we count ourselves doubly fortunate, and greatly indebted to him.

We are most grateful to Winifred Scholfield for making the drawings in the text. The jacket was the work of Isobel Brett and Margaret Wyn Williams, based on an early eighteenth-century oil painting of the City in the Salisbury Museum. Those who have been good enough to allow their possessions to be photographed or their photographs to be reproduced, have assisted in making this representative collection of plates possible. We thank them for their kindness. Separate acknowledgments are given in the list of plates. It has not been possible to name all the others who, by information, skill, or hard work, have assisted in the production of this book and merited our warm gratitude, but for much similar help, as well as patience and sound advice, it would be discourteous not to mention, collectively, Phoenix House.

Salisbury, 1957   HUGH SHORTT

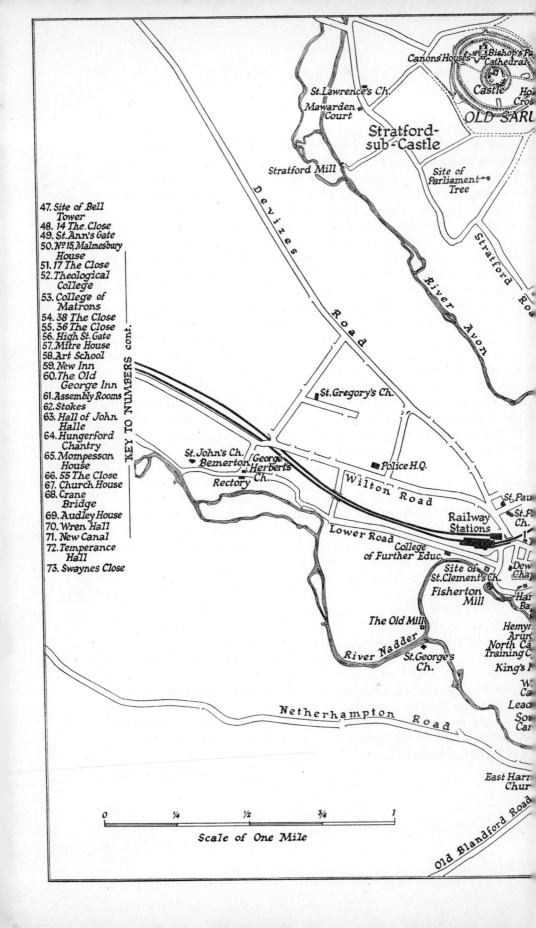

KEY TO NUMBERS cont.

Canons' Houses
Bishop's Pa
Cathedral
Castle
Ho
Cros
St.Lawrence's Ch.
OLD SARU
Mawarden
Court
Stratford-
sub-Castle
Stratford Mill
Site of
Parliament
Tree
Devizes
River Avon
Stratford Roa

St.Gregory's Ch.

St.John's Ch.
Bemerton
George
Herbert's
Ch.
Rectory
Police H.Q.
Wilton Road
St.Pau
St.P.
Ch.
Railway
Stations
Lower Road
College
of Further Educ.
Dew
Cha
Site of
St.Clement's Ch.
Fisherton
Mill
Har
Ba
Hemyr
Arun
North Ca
Training C
King's
W.
Ca
Lead
So
Car
The Old Mill
River Nadder
St.George's
Ch.
Netherhampton Road
East Harr
Chur
Old Blandford Road

0   ¼   ½   ¾   1

Scale of One Mile

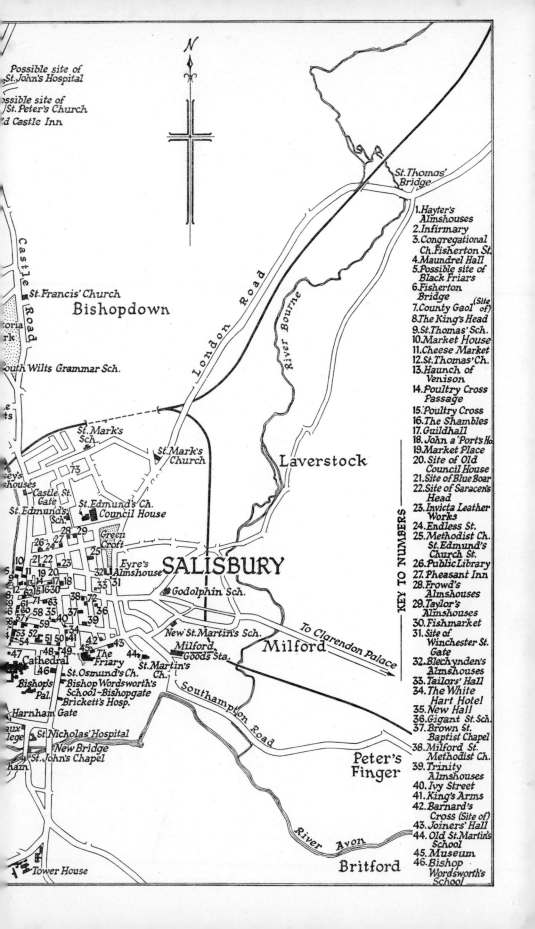

Possible site of
St. John's Hospital
Possible site of
St. Peter's Church
d Castle Inn

N

St. Thomas'
Bridge

Castle Road
St. Francis' Church
Bishopdown
South Wilts Grammar Sch.

London Road

River Bourne

Laverstock

St. Mark's Sch.
St. Mark's Church

73

sey's houses
Castle St. Gate
St. Edmund's Sch.
St. Edmund's Ch.
Council House
28 29
26 27
24
25
10
21-22 23
11 19 20
13 14 17 18
12 51 16 30
61-71 63
62
60 58 35
59
57
53 52
54 51 50 41
47
48 49 45
The Friary
Cathedral
46
St. Osmund's Ch.
Bishop's Pal.
Bishop Wordsworth's
School~Bishopgate
Brickett's Hosp.
Harnham Gate
eaux lege
St. Nicholas' Hospital
New Bridge
St. John's Chapel
ham

Green Croft
Eyre's Almshouse
32
33 31
38 72
37 36
40 34
39
42 43
44
New St. Martin's Sch.
Milford Goods Sta.
St. Martin's Ch.

SALISBURY
Godolphin Sch.

Milford
To Clarendon Palace

Southampton Road

Peter's Finger

River Avon

Britford

Tower House

KEY TO NUMBERS

1. Hayter's Almshouses
2. Infirmary
3. Congregational Ch. Fisherton St.
4. Maundrel Hall
5. Possible site of Black Friars
6. Fisherton Bridge
7. County Gaol (Site of)
8. The King's Head
9. St. Thomas' Sch.
10. Market House
11. Cheese Market
12. St. Thomas' Ch.
13. Haunch of Venison
14. Poultry Cross Passage
15. Poultry Cross
16. The Shambles
17. Guildhall
18. John a 'Port's Ho.
19. Market Place
20. Site of Old Council House
21. Site of Blue Boar
22. Site of Saracen's Head
23. Invicta Leather Works
24. Endless St.
25. Methodist Ch. St. Edmund's Church St.
26. Public Library
27. Pheasant Inn
28. Frowd's Almshouses
29. Taylor's Almshouses
30. Fishmarket
31. Site of Winchester St. Gate
32. Blechynden's Almshouses
33. Tailors' Hall
34. The White Hart Hotel
35. New Hall
36. Gigant St. Sch.
37. Brown St. Baptist Chapel
38. Milford St. Methodist Ch.
39. Trinity Almshouses
40. Ivy Street
41. King's Arms
42. Barnard's Cross (Site of)
43. Joiners' Hall
44. Old St. Martin's School
45. Museum
46. Bishop Wordsworth's School

I

A CITY THAT IS SET ON A HILL

From the earliest times to 1220

HISTORIANS of the Middle Ages were content to regard the remains of former times as the marvellous works of God, or of the giants who once lived in Albion. This childlike faith was supplanted from the sixteenth to the eighteenth century by a spirit of inquiry, which led to a more accurate description of earthworks and ruins in the English countryside, and a search among earlier writers for suggestions as to their origin. Only in the last hundred years has scientific excavation brought the truth within reach, so that prehistory can be recorded, and history illustrated, with a wealth of detail once considered beyond recall, or at best supplied by the over-fertile imagination of such men as William Stukeley. Yet with the gradual perfecting of this science something is inevitably lost, for interest is awakened as much by the search for knowledge as by the attainment of it, and even the Golden Road to Samarkand might be less alluring were that city more accessible.

The hill-fortress of Old Sarum, encircled by its deep rampart and crowned by its Norman motte, attracted Constable by its form (Pl. 1), and attracts us also by its mystery. As it has been excavated only in part, there is still room here for conjecture, and the historian must draw largely upon former writers and sift truth from falsehood as best he can. The contribution of field archaeology is still very small at this site, which played a considerable part in the life of the neighbourhood for some fifteen hundred years.

The story must begin somewhere in the Early Iron Age, that period of upheaval and sudden incursion which preceded the Roman conquest, but the few finds of this period do not suggest a very early date within it. To judge from better-explored sites in the neighbourhood one may guess that the first men, who put a bank and a ditch round this northern spur of Bishop Down, were the rusticated descendants of those adventurers who had settled many years before at All Cannings Cross and other places in Wiltshire. The reason was surely to protect the Avon crossing below the hill at Stratford, on a route which was important long before the Romans built straight roads.

Looking south, past the cathedral spire, Clearbury stands out on the horizon, and the map shows that other camps, Figsbury, Ogbury, Yarnbury, and the settlements south of the Wylye were all within reach by signal of Old Sarum at the centre. These people knew the danger of isolation in defence.

It is a point for future historians to decide whether this place formed a permanent settlement or merely a refuge for surrounding farmsteads like those on Boscombe Down, at Highfield, or at Woodbury. Only one refuse pit, considered to be of this period, was discovered during the excavations of 1909–15. It may be that Old Sarum was occupied in turn by traders from the west, well known from their lake villages at Glaston-bury and Meare, and then by the more warlike Belgae. The former are indicated by a bronze belt-link of pleasing lunate design, and the latter by pottery, bronze brooches, and coins of two of their kings, Tasciovanus and Cunobelin. History was still silent, and the informant of Hecataeus of Abdera, who seems to have described Stonehenge to this Greek geographer of the fourth century B.C., said nothing about Old Sarum, though he probably passed by it. Perhaps it was not yet built.

Although Britannia was a province of the Roman Empire from the first century until the fifth, Old Sarum is only mentioned in two late classical works, the Antonine and Ravenna Itineraries, under the name Sorbiodunum, evidently a latinization of the British name of which the meaning is obscure. It may mean 'the hill-fort by the sluggish river' or words to that effect. The identification of the place with Old Sarum seems to be reliable. Possibly Sorbiodunum was one of the twenty British towns captured by the young commander Flavius Vespasian, in his campaign towards the west, but here we are guessing, and once again we must look at the countryside and the man-made products, long concealed but finally brought to light, in order to reconstruct this long stretch of local history.

The only recognizable Roman features are the roads which run from northeast to southwest and from east to west; that is, from Silchester to Dorchester and from Winchester to a lost port on the Severn Sea. These two roads, and perhaps a British trackway running north and south, crossed at Old Sarum and are still to be seen from the ramparts making for the horizon in their various directions. Certain stretches of the roads are in use to this day.

The exact position of the Roman settlement has been a matter of controversy since the eighteenth century, when it was shown on a map to the south of the hill. A recent excavator thought it was to be sought at Stratford-sub-Castle. Neither suggestion is confirmed by finds and one may yet wonder if it were not built on Bishop Down, but excavation may show that it was superimposed on the British village within the ramparts. Certain it is that half-way down a well in the Norman motte foundations thought to be of Roman date were discovered on the original surface of the hill, composed of flint and ashlar, and overlying the refuse pit already mentioned. Some day no doubt we shall know whether this was the Forum or a barracks, or the corner of a square temple like that built on Maiden Castle, long after the inhabitants had moved down to Dorchester,

FIG. 1. The Wilton bowl

where there were hot baths and central heating. At the close of 1950 traces of Roman habitation were found in a field at Stratford near the line of the Port Way, and, more recently still, further Roman remains have come to light in Paul's Dene Estate on Bishop Down.

Long before Britain had ceased to be coloured purple on the Imperial map, it would appear that Old Sarum, with Wiltshire as a whole, had fallen to, and perhaps been retaken from, barbarous nations who attacked her from nearly every point of the compass. Evidence for this is forth-coming from Bokerly Dyke, the great defensive work along the Dorset border. This dyke was built in the first half of the fourth century and cut straight across the Roman road. In more settled years, however, the road was repaired and traffic resumed. Yet once again the barbarians arrived in force and the dyke was again thrown across the road, which remained closed until long after the last Roman soldier had crumbled in his grave.

The fifth century can hardly have been a pleasant period in which to live in Britain, for law and order had left the land only to be temporarily restored by such shadowy heroes as Aurelius Ambrosius and his general Arthur. Yet in isolated places a vestige of Roman culture seems to have survived, for in a Roman villa near West Dean were found bronze buckles of German origin which belong to this time. It is also tempting to attribute the bronze hanging bowl (Fig. 1) found at Wilton about 1860 to this fleeting period of British revival, but whether or not it indicates a community of the Celtic Church, there is not room here to discuss. Of Old Sarum itself we know next to nothing. The name Caer Caradoc—City of Caratacus—gleaned from the *Historia Britonum*, has been applied to it, but with little reason. A modern writer on the other hand has considered it a nodal point of British defence against the Anglo-Saxons.

If, for want of a better authority, we may trust the *Anglo-Saxon Chronicle*, we may believe that about the turn of the sixth century the foundations of

B

the West Saxon kingdom were laid by an invasion from the South Hampshire shore. Cerdic, the leader of this mixed host, fought the Britons at Charford, near Downton, in 519, but not until thirty-three years later, in 552, did his son Cynric capture Old Sarum. We have here a strong indication, from a Saxon source, of British resistance. The

FIG. 2. King Ethelwulf's ring

Saxons called the place Searoburh, derived from the British name, but with a new meaning, 'town' or 'place of battle', just as Halfaya in North Africa became Hellfire to the British of another age.

While the Saxons were enlarging and consolidating their new western kingdom, urban life decayed, for the Saxons were fighters and farmers rather than merchants, and we must suppose that Old Sarum too was left to crumble. Cemeteries of the period of the conquest have been found at West Harnham, at Petersfinger, and in the grounds of the present Council House, but not at Old Sarum itself. Stories which connect the names of Ina, Egbert, and even that of Alfred with the place must be discounted, since the documents supposed to substantiate them are not now traceable, if indeed they ever existed. The last-named king is said to have ordered Earl Leofric to refortify the stronghold against an expected attack by the Danish army, and though this story cannot now be proved, it was shown by excavation that the ramparts were in fact re-dug at some period before the Norman conquest, and the emergencies of Alfred's time may well have caused the reoccupation of this ancient fortification. It would be safer to deduce from the evidence of a gold ring (Fig. 2), decorated in niello work with the name of Alfred's father Ethelwulf, and found in a Laverstock cart-rut in 1780, that its owner was at least a visitor to this neighbourhood, where he was so unfortunate as to lose this beautiful ring.

The story that Edgar once held his court at Old Sarum is supported by Geoffrey Gaimar, who wrote about the middle of the twelfth century, but the circumstance of the king's sending one of his thanes to be killed in battle so that he might marry his widow is out of keeping with Edgar's character, and Geoffrey, who wrote in rhyming Norman-French verse, may have preferred a good story to historical accuracy. Elsewhere he confuses Old Sarum with Sherborne, so it is permissible to doubt his authenticity.

By the reign of Ethelred the ill-advised, we have tangible proof of the town's growing prosperity, in the form of silver pennies, which continued to be struck here until the time of Henry II. Also in Ethelred's unhappy reign Searoburh occurs for the second time in the pages of the *Anglo-Saxon Chronicle* for the year 1003. The Danish king Sweyn was busy avenging Ethelred's massacre of Danes on St Brice's day 1002 by attacking the West Country from the sea. After destroying Exeter, he marched inland and burnt Wilton, finally paying Sarum an unwelcome visit before returning to his fleet. Another writer says that Sarum too was burnt. Canute inherited the English possessions of his father Sweyn during Ethelred's lifetime and continued to harass the English. There is no early authority for the story that he too captured Sarum, but that he plundered some part of Wiltshire in the year 1015 is recorded in the *Chronicle*.

Although we have no more pre-Conquest records of the Saxon Searoburh, we learn from the *Chronicle* that Edward the Confessor stayed in the neighbouring village of Britford during the year 1065, where he conferred with Harold's brother the Earl Tostig. Old Sarum was only to achieve ecclesiastical and military importance as the Norman Salesberia in the reign of William the Conqueror.

Before passing on to the Norman phase of our story, something must be said of the position of Wilton, earlier mentioned as a possible centre of the Celtic Church in post-Roman times. From an ecclesiastical and political aspect her importance outweighed that of Salisbury until the reign of the Conqueror, while economically she predominated until Bishop Bingham built Ayleswade Bridge in 1244, and thus diverted trade from Wilton to New Sarum.

It has long been realized that Wilton was probably one of the earliest capitals of the West Saxon kings, and the chief town of the Wilsaetas. A minster (ministry) of the West Saxon church was established here as well as a royal palace, and from the eighth century until the Dissolution the Abbey of Nuns, first secular, then Benedictine, was one of the most important in the land. The Saxon seal of the Abbey, bearing the effigy of St Edith, a natural daughter of King Edgar, survives in a number of impressions, though the matrix has been lost.

On the ordinary man in the field the Norman Conquest can have had little immediate effect. He remained an Anglo-Saxon, with a cousin of the late King Edward the Confessor, of blessed memory, upon the throne which the Earl Harold had bravely occupied for a few months in 1066. Yet changes were soon to follow which could at least be seen and heard in the countryside. Culture became largely French, and as most of the

Saxon nobles were replaced by Normans, this culture permeated the land. French became the language of the court and of officialdom, and within a century churches built in the massive Norman style were to be seen in nearly every parish.

At Old Sarum, Godric worked in the mint for William the Conqueror, as he had worked for Edward, and the urban population continued to spread into suburbs outside the east and west gates, but there was still no cathedral nor even a castle. These two innovations are of Norman date and indicate the growing importance of the town. It was William's policy that cathedrals should be established in the more prosperous towns, but in ordering Bishop Hermann to transfer his see from Sherborne to this windy hill, he was probably considering a central site for the united dioceses of Ramsbury and Sherborne which the Bishop had been holding in plurality, and also the fact that the manor of Saris, berie already belonged to the Bishop. It is not improbable that the castle, a wooden structure dominating the town on its central motte, was erected before the cathedral. We should otherwise have expected the cathedral to occupy the central position. Nothing, however, is known of the first castle except that it belonged to the King. Possibly it was built by Edward the Sheriff, who is mentioned in Domesday, and was the grandfather of Earl Patrick. No doubt it was also by royal command that the outer rampart was again re-dug at about this time, and a stone curtain wall built upon it to surround the town (Pl. 2).

Hermann arrived in 1075, to build a cathedral, as it were, within a fortress, and thus set in motion a train of events which showed that the city was from that time divided against itself—a division which led to its deathblow in the thirteenth century, though not until 1832 was it finally interred. The interests, so often opposed to one another, were the royal authority, represented by the castellan and garrison of the castle, the ecclesiastical and manorial authority unified in the person of the bishop, and the civic and commercial interests of the citizens, hardly noticeable at Old Sarum, but playing an ever more dominant part after the foundation of the Newer City.

Hermann was a native of Lorraine, or Lotharingia, where he seems to have won the favour of the exiled prince, Edward the Confessor. When Edward returned to England in 1041, he brought Hermann as his chaplain and gave him rapid advancement. Hermann survived his move to Old Sarum by less than three years, yet he seems to have been the designer of the new cathedral there, which it fell to his successor, St Osmund, to complete (Fig. 3). This cathedral was a small basilica with an eastern apse and transeptal towers, indicated by the great thickness of their walls, of which the foundations survive. These towers also had small apses. This form of church is rare in England, but less so in eastern France and the Rhineland, and Hermann may have been copying the church at Compiègne or at Murbach when he designed his new cathedral.

FIG. 3. St Osmund's Cathedral

This basilica was, however, short-lived, for the day following the consecration ceremonies it was struck by lightning and the eastern part was
damaged beyond repair.

Immediately to the north of the transept a substantial oblong building
lay east and west. Massive remains of its crypt, vaulted upon a central
arcade, remain to be seen, and again the thickness of the walls suggests a
building of some height. Archaeologists have assigned it to the period
between the partial destruction of the cathedral and its rebuilding by
Bishop Roger. The purpose of this building is unknown, but as its
remains are more substantial than are others in the cathedral area, it is
tempting to consider it 'a chapel of our Lady yet standing and main-
teynid', as Leland found it in 1540. We may mention Ely cathedral as
one with a Lady chapel in a similarly detached position. It is unusual to
find a Lady chapel in a church already dedicated in honour of Our Lady,
as was Old Sarum Cathedral, but we have noticed that the chapel to
which we refer was erected at a time when the cathedral was largely
destroyed, and perhaps unusable, and it may have preserved the dedication
at Old Sarum long after the cathedral was dismantled.

St Osmund, successor to Bishop Hermann, through his writings, laid
the foundation of the *Sarum Use*, the application of which was to elevate
Salisbury to be one of the greatest dioceses in western Christendom. He
was the author of the *Institucio Osmundi* and the *Charta Osmundi*. In these
works he regulated the administration of his cathedral by four principal
persons, the dean, the treasurer, the chancellor, and the precentor. A
sub-dean and a succentor were also to be appointed, and the chapter was
composed of secular canons, the bishop himself being one. The *Consuetudinary*, or corpus of customs that developed from and arose out of

St Osmund's Charter, included ritual and ceremonial as well as con-stitutional regulations, but this book of customs grew up over a period of two or three centuries. The *Sarum Use*, as these writings were afterwards called, was soon adopted by many dioceses, not only in the British Isles but also in parts of western Europe.[1]

St Osmund was the founder of a library for his cathedral, and he is credited with writing and binding some of the books himself.[2] No fewer than sixty-five books of the library formed by him or added soon after his death still survive, and of these fifty-one are in the present Cathedral Library.

St Osmund died in 1099, and was succeeded by the more worldly Bishop Roger, a man of humble birth but of considerable capacity and unbounded ambition. Like Osmund, he was a Norman by birth. Finding favour with Henry I, he became chaplain to the king, and returning to England with him was made chancellor. In 1102 he was appointed to the bishopric of Salisbury, and became justiciar not long afterwards. It is, however, his work as a builder which chiefly interests us here. William of Malmesbury notes his ambition to be the greatest builder of his time and remarks in another place that the ashlar stonework erected by him was so faultless that it appeared to be carved out of solid rock.

The rebuilding of the ruined cathedral of Old Sarum was probably his first undertaking. Using the Abbaye aux Dames at Caen as his model, he added a pair of western towers to the original nave and entirely rebuilt and greatly enlarged the eastern end of the church. A central tower and aisled transepts were built instead of the transeptal towers, and the new choir and presbytery, similarly aisled, almost equalled the nave in length (Fig. 4). The excavators of the cathedral found sufficient remains of the floor to reconstruct nearly the whole design. This was a pattern in white Chilmark and grey-green Hurdcott stones, laid down in alternating strips to form long lines, lozenges, or chequers in various parts of the church. Roger's cathedral was to some extent glazed with coloured glass, a fact which is attested by many fragments found on the site by the excavators and preserved in the Salisbury Museum. Two small circular panels, thought to come from Old Sarum, have been incorporated in part of a window in the nave of the present cathedral made up of early glass. They represent the Annunciation (or perhaps the Angel appearing to Zacharias) and the Adoration. A large cloister occupied the area north of the chancel, and north of this again, up to the curtain wall, he built his palace, with living-rooms in a western

---

[1] The subject is more fully discussed in the Postscript.

[2] Another scholar, this time a true native of Salisbury, might receive honourable mention here. This is John of Salisbury, born shortly before 1120, who became a great author and one of the foremost Latin scholars of medieval times. Afterwards Bishop of Chartres, he was a close friend and supporter of St Thomas Becket, whose biography he wrote.

wing and the great hall and kitchen to the east, connected by a passage along the north wall of the cloister. A building which may have been the old palace was removed in the process. Houses for the canons were built opposite the west front of the cathedral, also backing on the curtain wall. In the angle between the chancel and the south transept was the canons'

FIG. 4. Bishop Roger's Cathedral

cemetery and a large cross. The tombs consisted of massive carved slabs covering stone coffins, of which one is preserved in the cloisters of the present cathedral. Two of these tombs commemorate Alward, whose name has not otherwise been preserved, and Godwin, the Precentor, who was living about 1160. Their epitaphs, carved on the coffin slabs, are in rhyming Latin hexameters. Most of these tombs were left undisturbed by the excavators.

Roger was not only concerned with ecclesiastical buildings; he gave full vent to his ambition in the erection of castles whose magnificence and strength were said to be unsurpassed in Europe. The castles of Sherborne, Malmesbury, and Devizes, as well as the central buildings in the castle at Old Sarum, were of his designing. The exact form of Roger's citadel upon the motte at Sarum is difficult to interpret, but a recent comparison with the better preserved remains of Sherborne Castle encourages the belief that the so-called 'keep' was a comparatively low building surrounding an open space, this space being filled with chalk up to the first-floor level of the eastern and southern wings, which are built on lower ground than those on the north and west. The chapel of St Nicholas occupied the southeast corner, and beyond the northern end of the east wing an apparently lofty but cramped tower, standing athwart the wall of the inner bailey, may have served both as a look-out and a dungeon.

Roger is not a character we can greatly admire. He betrayed the dynastic cause of Henry I, to whom he owed so much, and later betrayed Stephen, when his star appeared to wane. It is not surprising therefore that his castles were seized by Stephen in 1139, and that Roger died in the same year 'from mortification rather than old age', as a chronicler describes it.

During a part of the struggle with Stephen, Salisbury was held for Matilda, the empress, by the castellan Patrick, whom she created Earl of Salisbury. It is possible that the castle remained in his possession after the compromise with Stephen and the accession of Henry II. If this is so, the next phase of building, which comprised a stone wall round the inner bailey with strong postern towers at the east and west gates, was the work of Patrick's son William, who did not die until 1196. These towers are the most complete parts of the citadel now surviving.

After the abandonment of the city in the years following 1220 the castle was maintained by the earls, who were then also sheriffs of the county, and by subsequent sheriffs. It was used partly as a place of defence, partly as the sheriff's office, and also as a prison. As late as the fourteenth century a hall was built on the south side of the inner bailey and a bake-house to the east of it. Of these, only minor vestiges remain.

As well as the chapels associated with the cathedral and the citadel, there were parish churches in or around Old Sarum, vanished for the most part, but of which records survive and foundations may yet be found by excavation.

Francis Price mentions a church of St James, monastic in the time of King Ina and later a parish church. The site was unknown, but Henry Wansey, in his map of Old Sarum (1819), shows the parish to have been situated outside the ramparts to the south. Price also mentions a nunnery of the Blessed Virgin Mary in the time of Ina, afterwards endowed by Edith, the queen of Edward the Confessor, the site of which was likewise unknown. The documentary authorities for these foundations in the Cotton and Bodleian collections cannot now be traced, and there is good reason to think that, if found, they would prove to be forgeries.

There is, however, good authority for the church of the Holy Rood or Holy Cross, which was probably a garrison church standing in the outer bailey of the castle, not far from, or even on top of, the east gate. It may have been this church which in the fifteenth century was described as the Royal Free Chapel in the castle. Another parish church of St Peter seems to have stood in the east suburb. Foundations were found in 1935 in the grounds of the Castle Inn, which were probably the remains of this church. There has been considerable confusion between these two churches, perhaps because both have been described as 'over' the east gate. The word 'over' could mean 'near'. In 1246 the former church, whether within the east gate or actually above it, had become ruinous, and the nave was ordered to be rebuilt. Leland claimed that he saw 'sum tokens' of another church in 1540, which could refer to the church of St Peter. He also writes: 'Yn the est suburbs was a paroch chirch of St. John and there yet is a chapelle standinge.' Leland relied largely upon hearsay, and he probably means the leper hospital of St John (marked on Wansey's map and on the Ordnance Survey six-inch map) in the east suburb, but of which the exact site is unknown.

The parish church of St Lawrence at Stratford-sub-Castle may be the descendant of the church in the west suburb, but being of late date and unmentioned in Domesday, this suburb was perhaps served by the cathedral.

The castle in the inner bailey and the cathedral with its surrounding close occupied the western half of the hill-top, being separated from the eastern half, which formed the outer bailey, by two walls, pierced by gates, running north and south of the central motte. The outer bailey probably contained many civic buildings as well as the church of Holy Cross, but as these would have been made largely of wattle and daub, or timber, nothing now remains above ground. Leland writes that in 1540 not a single house remained either within or without the ramparts, though from this statement Stratford-sub-Castle must be excepted. Wansey records that the building in the east suburb now known as the Old Castle Inn was not erected before the end of the seventeenth century. He states that Mawarden Court in Stratford-sub-Castle was formerly the deanery, and that the subchantry or succentor's house, to the north of it, was still standing when he wrote. His statement, almost certainly inaccurate in detail, receives partial support from history, and also from the fact that Norman carved stones have been found incorporated in modern buildings in the village, though these may of course have been brought down from the hill. To this day there is a mill at Stratford which probably stands on the site of one of the four mills mentioned in Domesday as belonging to the Manor. The others may have been as far afield as Woodford or Harnham.

We are perhaps on surer ground if we believe an ancient tradition that the Parliament Tree, which stood on the south side of the fortress towards New Sarum, and under which the members for the rotten borough were elected, marked the site of the market square and perhaps a Town House. The tree itself was cut down more than a hundred years ago, and its position is indicated by a standing stone. Near this place were fields known as Burgage Tenure Lands, suggesting that on the south side, at least, the east and west suburbs had grown and perhaps united.

Bishop Roger, in his relations with the citizens, whose overlord he was, shows in a better light than he does in his political activities, for he granted them certain rights and privileges, such as an annual fair and freedom from tolls, though in later years the burgesses were to complain that the markets of New Salisbury were encroaching upon the trade of the old city.

The seeds of discord which led to the removal of the cathedral from Old Salisbury have already been mentioned. The name Vetus Sares-berie occurs as early as 1187, so that we may be sure that a New Salisbury was springing up before that date, probably during the episcopacy of Jocelin de Bohun, who succeeded Roger. It was, however, Bishop Herbert Poore who decided that his see should be transferred to the new city, and not until 1219, when his brother Richard Poore held the see, was permission for the move granted by Pope Honorius III. The papal letter survives, and records the many grievances under which the clergy and townspeople suffered. These were as follows: Being situated in a fortress, the church was subject to such inconvenience that the clergy could not remain there without danger to their persons. The church was exposed to such winds that those celebrating the divine offices could hardly hear each other speak. The fabric was so ruinous that it was a constant danger to the congregation, which had dwindled to the extent when it was scarcely able to provide for the repair of the roofs, constantly damaged by the winds. Water was so scarce that it had to be bought at a high price, and access to it was not to be had without the licence of the castellan. People wishing to visit the cathedral were often prevented by guards from the garrison. Housing was insufficient for the clergy, who were therefore forced to buy houses from laymen. Because of these and other grievances, permission for the removal was granted. This took place in the following year, and William de Wanda the Dean has described it in detail.

The old cathedral stood for another hundred years, but was pulled down by permission of Edward III in 1331, so that its stones might be used for building a wall round the Close in the new city, and there many of its carved stones are still to be seen. The tombs of three of the bishops, Osmund, Roger, and Jocelin, were removed to the new cathedral, possessions of pride and great interest.

The fate of the castle is more obscure. In 1152 Stephen had ordered Earl Patrick to destroy Roger's building, and this work was probably carried out in part, as fourteenth-century walls have been found overlying those of the twelfth century at foundation level. We have seen, however, that new and stronger defences were already being constructed later in the twelfth century, and these probably remained in use long after the city had been deserted, in fact until the advent of artillery reduced the security of stone walls and brought many castles into disrepair and disuse. It is thought that a temporary mint was established there during Charles I's civil war, but whatever was then standing was largely removed for building purposes soon afterwards, and today only foundations remain, under the care of the Ministry of Works.

The history of Old Sarum as a rotten borough belongs to another place, but before dismissing it let us remember that William Pitt first sat in the House of Commons as the member for Old Sarum. The place was bought by the Pitts largely from the Cecil family, late in the seventeenth century, for £1,500 and sold by them in 1805 to Lord Caledon for £65,000. The Old Sarum Volunteers and the Old Sarum Archers were institutions of the late eighteenth and early nineteenth centuries, without any real connections with the ancient borough.

Antiquarian research in the old city has so far been of a very limited extent. In 1795 steps leading to a subterranean chamber were discovered in the outer bailey north of the inner ditch. It was thought to be a 'sally-port', or a dungeon below a vanished Court of Justice. In 1815 the earth above caved in, and the true position of the steps is not at present known. Henry Hatcher, the historian, often quoted in these pages, surveyed the remains of the cathedral as they appeared on the surface, and tried his hand at excavation in 1834. It is curious that he is supposed to have found the finest piece of carving that has ever appeared at Old Sarum. It is a part of a double (or possibly quadruple) capital carved in a hard grey foreign stone, richly decorated with a design markedly similar to that found on the tomb of Gundrada de Warenne at Lewes, and also on a number of fragments at Glastonbury Abbey.

More extensive excavations were undertaken from 1909 to 1915 by the Society of Antiquaries, under the direction of Sir William Hope, assisted by Colonel W. Hawley, Duncan Montgomerie, and others. These excavations were confined to the areas of the cathedral and the inner bailey, and cannot be considered in any way complete. The finds are to be seen in the Salisbury Museum and in the small lapidarium on the site of the castle. Further and more complete investigation, which was intended before the second world war, is still awaited.

Meanwhile we must return to the thirteenth century, and the birth of the daughter city.

II

THE CREATIVE YEARS

1220–1535

'A CATHEDRAL to build and a city to found'—this was the vision splendid granted to Bishop Richard Poore and his architect Elias de Dereham. Long before the sixteenth century, Salisbury's cathedral and city were known throughout western Europe—the one for its beauty and the other for its trade. The medieval history of Salisbury is mainly concerned with the activities of its two great squares—the Close and the Market—and with the conflicts that broke out between them. Today the two squares survive. They still display their medieval parentage, although the intervening generations have implanted characteristic features of their own. And, while no longer in conflict, they still exemplify two differing aspects of human progress.

The day on which the foundation stone of the cathedral was laid— 28 April 1220—was the birthday of Salisbury. The events on the meadow of Myrfield must have been watched with very great interest, not only by those directly concerned but also by the folk from Fisher Town, from Harnham, and from the 'Old Town', a community of dwellings in the neighbourhood of Milford Hill, near to the present St Martin's Church. There is some evidence that prior to 1220 there were buildings on the episcopal lands to the south of Old Sarum. If that were so, new and old were woven together into one design in the years that followed. The present green-walled space around the cathedral, the arrangement of the Close houses, the gateways, the squares or chequers of the streets, the stone bridges, and the old churches, all afford plentiful justification today for terming Salisbury one of the most truly medieval of English cities. 'Building' was the operative word in the thirteenth century; and it was building not only in stone, timber, clay, and wattle. The cathedral organization was already adult, having for two hundred years followed the 'Use' of its great Father in God, Bishop Osmund. But the city was another story: here all the growing pains of youth and conflicts of adolescence had to be resolved, for civic life had been in its infancy in the city on the hill.

In 1227 Henry III gave Salisbury its first charter. It was declared a free city for ever, under the lordship of the bishop. Its citizens were to possess the same rights of trade and freedom for the conveyance of their goods as were enjoyed by the citizens of Winchester. Privileges which had been accorded to Old Sarum were to be affirmed for the new city, among them a weekly market and an annual fair. The bishop was empowered to strengthen the town by enclosing it with 'competent ditches'. He was also given the right—full of trouble for later years—of raising a tallage, or reasonable aid, from his tenants whenever the king found it necessary to tax the royal demesnes. The chief citizens of Salisbury formed a Merchant Guild, and this became the commune or civic body acting always under the control of the bishop.

The town made remarkable commercial progress. To it came the Plain's wealth of wool, and when in 1244 Bishop Bingham, Poore's successor, built Harnham Bridge, or, to give it its old and very picturesque name, Ayleswade Bridge, new avenues for trade were opened. The great western road ran from Old Sarum through Bemerton and Wilton. Bishop Bingham diverted it when he built across the Avon to the south of the city a bridge of six great arches of stone, 'a mayne and stately thing', says Leland. He continues: 'the chaunging of this way was the totale cause of the ruine of Old Saresbyri and Wiltoun. For afore this Wiltoun had a 12 paroch churches or more, and was the heade town of Wileshir.'

But Wilton's loss was Salisbury's gain; and vigorous use she made of it. Today the vicinity of Ayleswade Bridge is of great interest. Bishop Bingham's engineers diverted the force of the river by cutting an additional channel and creating a little artificial island, St John's Isle, upon which one pier of the bridge rests. A secondary bridge carries the road past the Hospital of St Nicholas. This foundation 'for the succour of poor and infirm persons' is mentioned in an extant deed of 1214, and it may owe its existence to Bishop Poore's zeal when he was still at Old Sarum. It was served by a semi-religious community of men and women, devout persons who sought through a fellowship of prayer and good works to relieve the social evils of their day. Their work of tending the sick and poor was particularly necessary in a neighbourhood where there were no monastic establishments nearer than Wilton or Amesbury. The hospital was richly endowed by Ela, Countess of Salisbury, one of the most saintly and public-spirited women of the thirteenth century, and it was enlarged and rebuilt by Bishop Bingham. In spite of much reconstruction a great deal of the ancient hospital can still be discerned. The main building was originally divided into two houses, each terminating at the east in a small chapel. In the southern aisle sick men were nursed where they could see the altar of St Nicholas. Sick women lay in the northern aisle below the altar of St Mary. In the fifteenth century the building became an almshouse. It managed to escape the fate of most religious houses at the time of the Reformation, probably because it had already acquired a lay master. In 1610 James I gave it a constitution which is still valid, and under which it has a master, chaplain, and means to maintain six poor infirm persons of each sex. These last, the Brothers and Sisters of St Nicholas, hold their places during the term of their lives, unless removed by the master, in accordance with the rules and constitution of the society. In the sixteenth century, married couples were eligible for admission, but, owing to the bad behaviour of one Nicholas Newton and his wife, who 'brawled at board and threw bones before all the company', the practice was discontinued. Salisbury may well be proud of possessing one of the oldest religious foundations in England, with an unbroken record of service.

Bishop Bingham entrusted the care of his bridge to the hospital, and for many years it adequately discharged this heavy and important duty. By Henry V's reign the bridge was urgently in need of repair, and, to defray the cost, the king authorized the levying of a toll for seven years on all merchandise taken across it. Since then the bridge has been widened, but the eastern side still shows the recesses which provided room and safety for pedestrians.

On St John's Isle stands the chapel of that name, built by Bishop Bingham. It has a very chequered history, but not even its modern transformation into a dwellinghouse can completely hide its old delineaments. At the east end are three lancet windows; at the west, a flight of stone steps replaces those which once led from the bridge to the chapel. Other lancet windows can be traced on the north and south. The walls are thick, made of plastered rubble, and the foundations are of solid masonry. This little chapel was closely associated with St Nicholas Hospital, the master and chaplain of which served its altar. Over the bridge linking hospital to chapel must have walked the russetclad priests two by two, and always in step, as stipulated by rule. It has another important association with the town. On Midsummer's Eve, 23 June, the Vigil of St John the Baptist, the members of the Tailors' Guild went in procession through the streets to the chapel of their patron saint.

Near by is another building once closely connected with the Hospital of St Nicholas. The interesting old house on the opposite corner, the walls of which are a medley of stone and flint, was once part of Salisbury's College of St Nicholas de Vaux (Pl. 3). The name 'de Vaux' is unusual. It originates from France, where the *Valli Scholares* were a community of divinity professors and students who had withdrawn from Paris in opposition to the new teaching of Schoolmen imbued with Aristotelian philosophy. In a secluded valley of the Auvergne, these exiles devoted themselves to the study of the Bible and the writings of the Fathers of the Church. Salisbury's College *de Valli Scholarum beati Nicholai* was founded by that shrewd and practical Bishop, Giles de Bridport, when plague and other troubles at Oxford were driving students from that educational centre. In 1238 scholars had been involved in an attack on the Papal Legate Otto. Thirty had been arrested and many more had fled to escape punishment. Some of the latter had come to Salisbury, where there was a Cathedral School of Theology under the direction of the chancellor. Affrays between students and citizens at Oxford led to a further exodus of scholars, and in 1261 Bishop Bridport seized the opportunity of providing 'poor, needy, well-born and teachable scholars' with a college at Salisbury. His foundation of 'de Valli' or, as it became, 'de Vaux', was the first University College to be set up in England. Many of the students divided their time between Salisbury and Oxford, where in due course, and on the recommendation of Salisbury's chancellor, who was in charge of their studies, they were granted their degrees. There may even have been a Salisbury Hall at Oxford where students from de Vaux resided. Lectures were given by members of the cathedral body and by qualified individuals resident in the city. This academic development was certainly in the tradition of a city whose name was known to every medieval scholar through the achievements of the great Osmund, Robert Grosseteste, and John, Bishop of Chartres. Nor were books lacking. Bishop Osmund's manuscripts formed the nucleus of a collection which grew steadily throughout the Middle Ages. A valuable addition to it came in the early fifteenth century when William Cyrcestre, a canon of the cathedral, presented all the manuscripts he had acquired in a lifetime of indefatigable search. The practice of storing books in chests and aumbry cupboards had obvious dangers and disadvantages, and in 1445 the cathedral chapter, inspired by the example of Hereford and by the work of Humphrey, Duke of Gloucester, at Oxford, decided to build a great gallery above the eastern walk of the cloisters. There the books were stored in the southern section, while the remainder of the gallery became the lecture room for the 'chancellor's schools'. Unfortunately the southern section was pulled down in 1756, to save the cost of repairing it, but for more than three hundred years it was the educational heart of Salisbury. The library remains in the northern section and contains some of the most precious manuscripts and books in Britain—among them many medieval liturgical books which are of great interest to all students of the Sarum Use, one of the four existing contemporary copies of Magna Carta, and some fine products of the early printing press.

De Vaux, nurtured in a lively intellectual atmosphere, grew and flourished. Its buildings followed the usual pattern of medieval academic halls of residence and formed a rectangular block. From the corner where the modern St Nicholas Road and de Vaux Road meet, its longer side stretched to the south gate of the Close, its shorter side towards Ayleswade Bridge. Hidden away from public view was a courtyard which gave access to the college rooms—a similar plan can be seen in many colleges at Oxford and Cambridge. De Vaux came to an end in Henry VIII's reign, and only the bits of old buildings incorporated into modern houses, a few fragments of old walls, and the house at the corner which might once have been the Porter's Lodge remain of Salisbury's once famous college (Pl. 4).

Two older educational establishments also flourished in medieval Salisbury, the Song School for the cathedral choristers and the Grammar School. The latter was situated next to the Bell Inn, and no trace of it remains. The Song School, now the Cathedral School and housed in what was once the Bishop's Palace, survives and prospers.

Among those who lectured to the students of de Vaux were Franciscan friars, many of whom were men of high intellectual attainment. An area still known as the Friary lies on the south side of St Ann Street. Here, between the years 1225 and 1228, a company of Grey Friars made their home. Is it too much to imagine that St Francis, still alive in Italy, realizing some of the difficulties likely to beset a community engaged in the gigantic task of building a cathedral and a city, gave his special blessing to the Salisbury mission? The friars were warmly welcomed by Bishop Poore, who lent them land on which to build their convent. The King, Henry III, gave generous grants of timber from the neighbouring forests. As the number of friars grew—there were twenty in 1243, forty-four in 1335—the wooden buildings, including a chapel dedicated to St John, were enlarged and rebuilt in stone, obtained by permission of Edward I from the broken-down walls of Old Sarum. With chapel, cloister, frater, chapter house, infirmary, gardens, and orchard, the original friary covered a large area. It was an important house in the Franciscan organization for southern England. For a short time it was the head of a 'custody', or group of houses, and when it was later incorporated in the London Province it was selected for the meetings of the provincial chapter in 1393 and in 1510. Richard II attended the 1393 meeting. He 'splendidly feasted the chapter of Friars Minor at Salisbury, and ate with them in the refectory, having with him Queen Anne, and Bishops, and other lords, on the feast of the Assumption of the Blessed Mary, and there he wore the regalia and crown'. It is pleasant to read of this luxurious break in the austere lives of the friars, whose staple fare consisted of barley bread, and beer so thick and bitter that it had to be diluted with water to be drinkable.

The value of their work during three hundred years of Salisbury's history cannot be overestimated. They had come to teach and to preach, to serve the poor, to help the sick. For their faithfulness in all their labours, the citizens expressed their gratitude to the brothers on more than one occasion. They were on excellent terms with the cathedral body and with the Dominican Friars who left Wilton for Fisher Town later in the thirteenth century.

In 1538 Royal Commissioners visited and examined both friaries, and both were dissolved in that same year although no complaints were made against either of them. Before the end of the sixteenth century a Salisbury merchant named William Windover acquired the Franciscan property. Today, behind the uninteresting façade of Windover House in St Ann Street, many remains of the old friary are carefully preserved. It is possible to see the refectory, the courtyard, and the well, and a wealth of old stone and timber has survived the changes and chances of more than four hundred years. Other remains of the Franciscan friary are probably incorporated in neighbouring houses and in the old buildings of the lane near by, once called Frerenstreet. Nothing remains of the Dominican friary which had been built by the side of the river on the site now occupied by the malt-houses in Fisherton Street. The Brothers Preachers were best known to the citizens through their sermons at the city crosses.

Thirteenth-century Salisbury had by no means exhausted its zeal for building with the Cathedral, St Nicholas Hospital, Ayleswade Bridge, St John's Chapel, the College of de Vaux, and the friaries—to say nothing of the domestic buildings which were springing up in the Close and along the streets. Much of the city's medieval glory is enshrined in its churches of St Martin, St Thomas, and St Edmund. The sixteenth-century antiquary Leland is responsible for some confusion that has arisen about the history of St Martin's. He reported that Salisbury had only two churches, St Thomas's and St Edmund's, and that there was an old barn standing to the north of St Nicholas Hospital which was all that remained of a church dedicated to St Martin. It is probable that Leland was confusing St Martin's Church with St John's Chapel. 'This Church', he writes, 'was profaned . . . it stood exceeding low and cold, and the river at rages came into it.' He adds vaguely that there was a new church dedicated to St Martin 'which in another place yet standeth' (Pl. 5). His omission of St Martin's from the city churches may be due to the fact that it stood a little beyond the ramparts. It possesses architectural features of earlier date than the cathedral, and was probably the church of that cluster of dwellings already referred to as 'The Old Town' of Milford. This lay on, or near, the ancient road from Clarendon to Southampton (St Martin's Church Street was once called Hampton's Way). In 1269 the church is mentioned as one of the three parish churches of New Sarum. With the city's growth it was enlarged and rebuilt, mainly in the fifteenth century.

The magnificent Church of St Thomas was founded about the same time as the cathedral and dedicated to that most revered of English saints, Thomas Becket. The first church was a wooden building, designed to meet the needs of a vast influx of people. Within ten years it was rebuilt in stone, and the remains of this thirteenth-century building can still be seen. But St Thomas's Church, like St Martin's, reached its full splendour in the fifteenth century, when the wealth of the trade guilds and the generosity of individual merchants gave it its splendid roof and south chapel (Pl. 9), and rebuilt the north chancel aisle as the Chapel of St George.

Today the church is full of interest, but there are two features in

c

particular which attract the notice of visitors, the Bell Tower and the great Doom painting over the chancel arch (Pl. 7). The tower was built in 1400, away from the church. It was incorporated with the main build-ing when the nave aisles were added in the second half of the fifteenth century. The Doom painting, the largest of its kind in England, is also

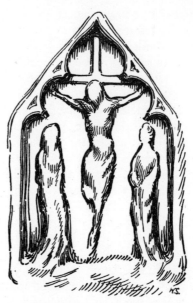

FIG. 5. Crucifixion, St Thomas's Church

fifteenth-century work. There is a tradition that it was painted to com-memorate the safe return of a pilgrim from the hazards of his journey. Certainly there is the figure of a pilgrim on the left of the painting. St Thomas's may have been the church visited by the men and women pilgrims who came from far and near to behold the wonder of the great cathedral spire added in the early fourteenth century. It is thought that the path that stretches round the church from Silver Street to Minster Street was a Pilgrims' Walk, and that the old Crucifixion (Fig. 5), still to be seen on the south wall, was placed near a box for their offerings. The southern churchyard, with the church and old tower on one side and picturesque houses, once timber-framed, now tiled in mellow brick, on two others, re-creates the medieval atmosphere better than any other locality in Salisbury. How beautiful one at least of those surrounding buildings must originally have been is shown by the exquisite woodwork of a small double light (Fig. 6) preserved in the house on the southwest corner.

St Edmund's Church was founded in 1269 by Bishop Walter de la Wyle as part of a college for twelve secular canons, and dedicated in

FIG. 6. Three medieval wooden window-frames

honour of Edmund of Abingdon, Archbishop of Canterbury and one-time Treasurer of Salisbury Cathedral. The church was originally an enormous building stretching almost to the railings of the present School Lane. What remains constitutes the choir of the old church to which a nineteenth-century chancel has been added. The rest of St Edmund's College—the residential quarters for the provost and canons—covered the site now occupied by the Council House.

The twentieth century, which finds it so hard to construct even little houses for its people and to which the building of a church is a major enterprise involving an alarming outlay of money, and an even more alarming uncertainty as to how it can be raised, must look back with wondering admiration at the almost incredible achievements of medieval Salisbury. How did it find all the material and money required? The cathedral stone came from the quarries of Chilmark, its marble from Purbeck—a twelve years' supply of it being freely given by Alice Briwere, lady of the manor of Worth Matravers—its oak timbers were a royal gift from the forests of Henry III. As for the homes of the people, it seems that some of the more substantial houses in Old Sarum were taken down and rebuilt in the new city. Materials for lesser homes were not hard to find. There was an abundance of flints, plenty of mud, good local deposits of clay, and all the wattle men could need on the trees by the rivers. Despite munificent gifts in kind, the cathedral could never have been built without money to pay craftsmen and labourers, and to provide yet more materials. In response to a widespread appeal contributions came from

far and near, from great landowners and from the faithful in other
dioceses, but the fact remains that without the steady giving throughout
the years by those most concerned—cathedral chapter and people of
Salisbury—the great buildings in the Close and City would never have
been completed. It must be remembered that giving 'for the glory of God'
was characteristic of this inspired and creative age, the fruits of which can
be seen not only in England but throughout western Europe. Salisbury
was unique only in having a completely new field for its activities. It was
a little place. Its population was small. But it possessed a religious fervour
out of all proportion to its size, and this, directed and controlled by master
minds, gave it its immense vitality and enterprise. Those were the days
when men believed that by investing their money in a 'treasury of good
works' they would build up a spiritual credit balance for the world to
come. Not that all the profit lay in the future—the church provided the
colour and the pageantry of everyday life. Churches had to be large to
allow for the processions of the solemn festivals. Products of craftsmen's
art in stone and wood, precious glass, rich priestly vestments, lights of
innumerable candles—these things met human needs as much as they
quickened spiritual aspirations.

It was indeed fortunate that the growth of the wool trade gave Salisbury's
citizens the money to spend. Bishop Bingham knew well, when he built
Ayleswade Bridge, that all the plans for the future of the city as a religious
and educational centre must be buttressed by the well-being of its civic
and economic life.

There was very little delay over municipal organization. A mayor is
first mentioned in 1261, and eight years later, when St Edmund's College
was founded, the city was divided into three parishes—St Martin's, St
Thomas's, and St Edmund's—each with carefully defined boundaries not
very different from those which exist today. Outside them lay the Close
and the little parish of St Nicholas. From the Merchant Guild, which
comprised the town's chief citizens, came the commune or corporation
nominally representative of the four wards into which the parishes were
divided for civic purposes. The commune consisted of two councils,
named, from the number of their members, the Twenty-four and the
Forty-eight. The Twenty-four were the aldermen, six from each ward.
The Forty-eight, twelve from each ward, were the 'assistants' of the
aldermen. There was nothing democratic, in the modern sense, about the
commune. Its members held office for life, and vacancies were filled by
co-option. Yet it was not oligarchic, for its powers were strictly limited
by episcopal control, and each of its members had to be acceptable to the
bishop, the city's feudal overlord. The bishop's will, approval or dis-
approval, was conveyed by his bailiff or steward, who always attended
commune meetings. He was treated with great respect as the most important person present, until clashes occurred between episcopal and
municipal rights. As for the mayor, bound as he was by a solemn oath of

FIG. 7. The Bishop's Guild Hall

loyalty and obedience to the bishop, he found his position increasingly difficult as time went on and claims for the city's independence grew with its wealth. Upon the commune rested responsibility for the town's security, law, and order, control of its markets, and all the regulations necessary for the preservation of health and general well-being. The city's charter gave it the right to hold a court of piepowders where, with the mayor as judge, disputes arising during markets could be settled on the same day as they occurred.

In 1295 Edward I summoned the Commons for the first time to attend Parliament. Salisbury was represented by two members chosen by the commune. It was not a highly sought honour, for the king called Parliament to whatever place, and at whatever time, best suited his convenience. During the Middle Ages it was found necessary to try, first, a system of punishment by fines for non-attendance, and, later, of reward by payment for attendance. Neither had any marked success. It must have been a great relief to local members when on the occasion of Richard II's visit to Salisbury in 1393 Parliament was summoned to meet in the hall of the bishop's palace.

For more than seven hundred years, Salisbury's civic administration has been localized in the southeast corner of the Market Square, where an eighteenth-century Guild Hall stands today. A guild hall (Fig. 7) stood on part of the same site in the thirteenth century, being one of the first buildings raised in the new city. It served as the meeting place of the commune, a court of justice, and a prison. Stocks and whipping post stood in the open square of the market, and here, too, gallows were erected when required. By the reign of Elizabeth the Guild Hall had become unsuitable for the civic and social functions of the City Fathers, and a new Council House was built near by. This was a four-storeyed wood-frame structure, surmounted by a lantern tower. Law and criminal courts were held on the ground floor, and the rooms above were used for business meetings and banqueting. Several private houses in the vicinity were rebuilt at about this time, among them a house in Fish Row built by Henry Serryge, wool merchant and Mayor of Salisbury in 1508. Its later demolition is to be regretted if the very fine stone chimney-piece (now in the Diocesan Finance Office) which was taken from it is any indication of the quality of the rest of the building. The chimney-piece bears Henry Serryge's initials and his merchant's mark.

From the beginning, the Merchant Guild of Salisbury was fully alive to the superiority of the new town over the old, from the point of view of trade. It had come into existence when a medieval industrial revolution was in progress, and when water-power was becoming an essential factor in the manufacture of cloth. The wealth of English wool merchants had been founded on the export demand for raw wool, which was collected in staple towns, sampled, weighed, and dispatched to special ports for shipment. Whether Salisbury was a staple town is uncertain, for its name does not appear in the lists of those towns. These lists, however, were not always complete, and Salisbury's proximity to the Plain, one of the greatest wool-producing areas in England, and the fact that the town possessed a Hall of the Staple in St Martin's Church Street, suggest the possibility that the city actually was a staple town. In the thirteenth century the export of raw wool was mainly to Flanders, where weaving and dyeing had become a fine art. Flemish cloth, woven from English wool, was imported into England. Before the end of the century Edward I had placed an embargo on the export of wool to Flanders, and had initiated the policy which, in the days of his grandson, Edward III, was to make England the centre of both wool and cloth trade.

The ramifications of the latter industry included spinning, weaving, dyeing, fulling, and cloth-finishing. Salisbury quickly identified itself with all these operations. It had abundance of raw wool and a plentiful supply of running water which was essential to the industry. The raw wool had to be washed, carded, and spun before it could be woven. Salisbury women did this preliminary work in their homes, most of it as a spare-time occupation between their domestic duties. There were few houses in the town without a spinning-wheel. After spinning came weaving—whole-time skilled work done by men. The steady, heavy thumping of working looms was once a familiar sound in Salisbury streets. Then came dyeing in steaming vats like great coppers, and after that the cleansing of the cloth in the fulling mills by the rivers. As near as possible stood the tenters, the wooden frames or racks on which the cloth was stretched and dried. Even then it was not finished—its nap had to be raised with teazles and then sheared with gigantic scissors until it was smooth.

Every street in the city was associated with some activity of the wool trade. Castle Street, where the backs of the houses on the west side stretch to the River Avon, was particularly concerned with weaving, dyeing, and fulling. Between the site of the old Castle Street Gate and the market (Pl. 8) there still remain at least a dozen narrow openings, once passage-ways between houses, allowing access from the street to the looms, dyeing-vats, and fulling-mills behind. To explore one or two of these alleys is to walk from our own time back into Salisbury's distant past, when medieval masters and journeymen plied their trade, and apprentice lads were taught the 'mistery' of their craft.

The Green Croft, once known as St Martin's Croft, was a rack close where cloth was stretched and dried. Other open spaces which were put to similar use have long since been covered with buildings. In the Butts beyond the Castle Street Gate men and lads gathered on Sundays after High Mass for the weekly archery practice that the law made compulsory.

Before the end of the fifteenth century Salisbury's textiles, particularly the fine flannels or 'motleys', had gained a widespread reputation. In addition to all the work involved by its own manufactures, the city supplied wool for the home market and exported surplus stock to such continental centres as were authorized by the Fellowship of the Staple, a company of three hundred leading English wool merchants who con-trolled the overseas wool-trade after 1346 from their headquarters at Calais. From Salisbury, raw wool was carried by pack-horses to South-ampton, Lymington, and Poole, shipped to Calais, and from there sent out to European markets, under licence of the Staple. Woollen cloth was similarly exported on an ever-increasing scale, for it was not subject to the heavy tax which restricted the sale of raw wool abroad. A number of Salisbury's wool merchants had the honour and distinction of serving as Merchants of the Staple. The houses of three of them survive, and provide substantial evidence of the wealth which the wool trade brought.

The picturesque old house of John a'Porte has looked up Butcher Row from Three Lyon Chequer for more than five hundred years. John a'Porte, Merchant of the Staple, six times Mayor of Salisbury, was de-scribed by his opponents as 'a man of evil disposition and great malice'. His building, however, was sound. Today it is a china shop, but it has suffered very little alteration in the course of centuries. William Webb, Merchant of the Staple, who, with John Halle, 'did buy up all the wool on Salisbury Plain', chose for himself a site removed from the turmoil of the town, with a garden sloping down to the Avon. Church House, as it is known today, has suffered many vicissitudes, but is still to be dis-tinguished by the beauty of its fine fifteenth-century building. The old hall or banqueting room has the original corbels of its vaulted timber roof, one of them bearing Webb's merchant's mark (Figs. 8 and 9). From the possession of the Webb family, the house passed to the Earls of Audley and Castlehaven. Then it fell upon evil days, until in the eighteenth century it became the Workhouse and Women's House of Correction

FIG. 8. Corbel in Church House (Webb Hall)

for the city. Today, as Church property, it is a carefully preserved reminder of the past, as well as a most useful diocesan centre.

As for the third merchant, John Halle, he was responsible not only for the well-known and magnificent Hall of John Halle, now incorporated into the Gaumont Cinema, but also for many troubled pages in Salis- bury's history of which more must be written later. Merchant of the Staple, shipowner at Southampton, four times mayor, Member of Parliament for the city, he is an outstanding example of a Salisbury man of affairs. His hall has a splendid roof of foliated woodwork, and three great mullioned windows filled with stained glass, some of it dating back to the fifteenth century. The stone chimney-piece with the arms and merchant's mark of John Halle is one of the treasures of the city. The external wall of the Hall, seen in the adjoining passage-way, provides an interesting study of building and building material. John a'Porte, William Webb, and John Halle must have known one another well (and one another's dining-halls) though William Webb was younger by many years than the other two.

No domestic building survives to remind men of William Swayne, another fifteenth-century wool merchant, the patron and benefactor of the Tailors' Guild. He has left his memorial in the beautiful south chapel of St Thomas's Church (Pl. 9), where his arms and merchant's mark can be seen on the shields of the roof, and in the old glass of the east window. Two chantry altars once stood in this chapel, one of the Blessed Virgin, and the other of St John the Baptist, patron saint of the Tailors. Both

FIG. 9. Webb merchant's marks

were richly endowed by William Swayne. His name lives in Swayne's Close, now a residential area on the northeast of the town, where his 'tenters' once stood.

While the woollen trade provided the main occupation of medieval Salisbury, all the other crafts existed which were essential to the town's economy: baking, brewing, building, tanning, and very many more. A building still called the Old Mill stands not far from St Thomas's Church, straddling the river. Today it generates electricity, but one of the bishop's mills recorded in Domesday Book stood upon this site. Ample evidence remains of the craftsmanship of the Joiners—the fellowship of the carpenters, builders, and other associated crafts. Their name is perpetuated by the Joiners' Hall in St Ann Street (Pl. 6). A vision of their crafts is vouchsafed sometimes today when a house is undergoing reconstruction. Timber framework and massive beams stand temporarily revealed to the passer-by, before being hidden behind stone, plaster, glazed tiles, or cement. In the Close, and in practically every street, there are houses with eighteenth- and nineteenth-century façades concealing far older structures within. Minster Street (Pl. 11), New Street, Crane Street, High Street, and St Ann Street provide many examples of buildings which have not yet been sacrificed to the demands of modern commerce and convenience. Often, alas, neglect has been allowed to speed decay, as in the Tailors' Hall (Fig. 10) in Milford Street. This was built by the munificence of William Swayne, in the locality once known as Swayne's Chequer.

Medieval Salisbury was as attractive as it was busy. As Richard Poore had planned, buildings were arranged in chequers or squares, with the streets running at right angles to one another. There were some twenty-two of these chequers. They derived their names from the chief hostelry or from the most important family living in the chequer. Blue Boar Row remains of what was once Blue Boar Chequer; Antelope Square is still a reminder of the old Antelope Chequer. There are modernized hotels bearing the names of old inns which once stood in White Hart Chequer and White Horse Chequer. Trinity Hospital still stands in what was once Trinity Chequer.

Many of the old streets carry their original names, but Minster Street

FIG. 10. West window of the Tailors' Guild Hall

once included the modern Castle Street, Silver Street, and High Street. In the thirteenth century the High Street stretched from Endless Street to St John's Street, and led into Drakehall, Dragenol, or Dragall Street—the modern Exeter Street. A wealthy Salisbury family called Drake built their Hall upon it, and gave it its name. (Under the pulpit in St Thomas's Church there is a grave slab with perfect lettering, inscribed to the memory of Dan Drake, aged eleven, son of Dan Drake, gentleman.) The years have played a game with Salisbury street names, but they have not changed their straight, uncompromising layout.

Down the chief streets there once ran a stream of water, with small stone or wooden bridges to allow for pedestrian crossings. The Milford Street stream was deep enough near the Red Lion to permit the use of a cage and ducking-stool for the punishment of scolds. Compared with most towns, Salisbury was, at this period, a clean and healthy place, free from the foul pest-ridden alleys of antiquity. No doubt some parts of the city were made unsavoury by the exigencies of trade. The canal, for instance, known for centuries as the Ditch, was in useful proximity as a dumping ground to the butchers of the shambles along Butcher Row, and to the fish vendors of the Fish Market. Names show that trades were localized in the city. Besides Butcher Row, Fish Row, Ox Row, and Oatmeal Row, which survive, there was a Wheelwrights' Row, a Cooks' Row, a Cordwainers' Row, an Ironmongers' Row, and a Smiths' Row. As well as the Wool Market, there was a Yarn Market and a Corn Market. The last was in Castle Street. The Yarn Market was held weekly round a very large elm-tree in the Market Place. This elm must have stood near, or on, the spot marked until June 1953 by Sidney Herbert's statue.

The four city crosses were centres for the preaching of Franciscan and Dominican Friars as well as for the sale of particular commodities. The Cheese Cross, where milk as well as cheese was sold, stood at the market end of Castle Street, still called the Cheese Market. The Poultry Cross, sole survivor of the four, and known also as the High Cross and the Green Cross, is first mentioned in 1335, and was used for the sale of poultry and vegetables. Bernewell's, or Barnewell's, Cross (now known as Barnard's Cross) was a Cattle Market. The Wool Cross stood in the Wool Market in the New Canal.

Most of the houses in the town had gardens, and there were many open spaces. The city authorities were insistent on the preservation of amenities. The water-channels in the streets had to be kept clean and undamaged. Owners of ducks, pigs, and geese had to keep them on their own premises. Cattle for sale must be kept 'in their proper place' near Barnewell's Cross and Culver Street. The 'abomination or filth' of slaughtering animals in the open street of Butcher Row was stopped in the reign of Henry VI. Later, the butchers were forbidden to cast entrails into the Town Ditch, or over Fisherton Bridge, 'except it be in the current or shower of the river, or else in the usual place down the stairs appointed'. (The passage-way to the 'usual place' was probably the one facing the New Canal, running alongside the present Woolworth building.)

The cathedral with its spire was the great magnet which attracted visitors to Salisbury. The Confraternity of Salisbury Cathedral was a highly prized association to which a number of very important people belonged. John of Gaunt, Henry Bolingbroke, Henry of Monmouth, Humphrey Duke of Gloucester, Joan, Queen of Henry IV, and Car-dinal Beaufort were among its members. The solemn services of admission to the Confraternity were occasions which filled the city with noble personages and their retinues.

Many inns were built to provide accommodation for these exalted visitors, and for the hundreds of other pilgrims to the cathedral. What is claimed to be a thirteenth-century inn survives in the Haunch of Venison in Minster Street, and an astonishing number of fourteenth- and fifteenth-century foundations continue to ply a brisk trade. History lives on in the Old George in High Street, which contains, so it is claimed, oak beams brought from Old Sarum. The Pheasant (Pl. 21), once known as the Crispin, in Salt Lane, is another ancient inn. It stands near the remains

of the Shoemakers' Hall. The King's Arms in St John Street dates from
the fifteenth century. Nothing, except the name, is left of the once famous
hostelry, the Blue Boar. Shakespeare in his *Richard III* stages one of his
shortest scenes in an 'open space' in Salisbury. In it the Duke of Bucking-
ham, caught in arms as a rebel against the King, is led to his execution.
There is much to support the local belief that the Duke was beheaded in
the yard of the Blue Boar Inn, now occupied by the premises of Style and
Gerrish. With its neighbouring inn, the Saracen's Head, the Blue Boar
was removed when the Market Place was widened early in the nineteenth
century. Gone, too, is the Lamb, which once stood on the New Street
corner of the High Street, on the site of a hut built as a temporary lodging
by Bishop Poore. Mitre House, which has replaced hut and inn, still
provides the robing-room for each new bishop prior to his enthronement
in the cathedral. The wooden framework of ancient windows (Fig. 6) on
the third storey has been uncovered during recent reconstruction. This
corner was once known as Florentine Corner. A possible reason is that
the Lamb, and another inn which stood where Beach's bookshop stands
today, were patronized by Lombard merchants and bankers whose
business took them to centres of the wool trade.

For very poor visitors there was Trinity Hospital. It stands today in a
quiet back street, a picturesque brick building round an open courtyard.
It was founded as an act of penitence by Agnes Bottenham in 1379. She
was the hostess of an ale-house, and had been the owner of a brothel on
the site of which the hospital was built. It gave a home, for the remainder
of their lives, to 'twelve poor persons, and food and shelter nightly for
twelve poor strangers, with liberty to tarry three days and three nights,
should any so desire'. Those who fell sick were to receive help and care
until they were restored to health. It had, and still has, a chapel and a
chaplain. Knowledge of Trinity Hospital spread all over England. In
ten bishoprics a forty days' indulgence was granted to penitents who gave
it charitable aid. Rich endowments were given to it in 1400 by John
Chandler, citizen of Salisbury, enabling it to have thirty beds 'for the
succour of the sick and poor daily resorting thither'. Its work is thus
eulogized in a fourteenth-century document: 'The seven works of mercy
were there fulfilled. The hungry were fed, the thirsty had drink, the naked
were clothed, the sick were comforted, the dead were buried, the mad
were restored to their reason, orphans and widows were nourished, and
lying-in women were cared for.' As an almshouse it survived the
Reformation. It was rebuilt in the eighteenth century (Pl. 10), and is now
one of the city almshouses for old men, administered by the Trustees
of the Salisbury Municipal Charities.

Salisbury opened its arms to rich and poor, and in return got wealth,
blessing, and a fair reputation. But it certainly was not an abode of peace.
From early days there were elements of unrest within the city, and from
outside came the bitter opposition of Wilton, which was threatened with

ruin by the growth of the new city. Old Sarum, too, the ancient mother on the hill, might have said with truth that her grey hairs were being brought to the grave by the activities of her daughter.

The trouble started soon after Salisbury had obtained its first charter in 1227. Old Sarum and Wilton complained that although the new city had been given the right to one weekly market, the bishop permitted several markets to be held, to the great detriment of their own trade. Wilton was particularly aggrieved, for her ancient rights not only gave her markets on Monday, Wednesday, and Friday, but freedom from all commercial competition within a reasonable radius. Twice in the reign of Edward II attempts to restrain Salisbury were made and ignored. It was not until 1361 that the controversy was settled: Wilton was to keep her markets; to Salisbury was conceded the right of holding market on Saturday as well as Tuesday; while Old Sarum had a Thursday market. Wilton could not always claim to be the innocent, injured party. Her bailiffs were accused of waylaying merchants bound for Salisbury and other places, and of compelling them to expose their goods in Wilton market. 'The bailiffs did beat them, ill-use them, and wound them, lead them like prisoners to the town and force them to stand there.' Salisbury still holds her market twice a week, but from Wilton the ancient commercial glory has departed, while Old Sarum has diminished to an interesting and romantic site, speaking only of the past.

Salisbury's growing wealth and the peaceful pursuits of its inhabitants early raised the problem of defence. Henry III had granted Bishop Poore the right to enclose his new city with 'competent ditches', but it is doubtful whether they were ever dug. The rivers provided a natural line of defence on the south and west. Ayleswade Bridge at Harnham, the Upper Bridge leading to the village of Fisher Town, and the Lower Bridge in Crane Street, were all thirteenth-century structures. (The Upper Bridge has been entirely rebuilt, and the other two considerably widened.) In time of danger they were key points of defence, and the responsibility of manning them belonged to specially appointed citizens. In the reign of Edward III, Bishop Wyvil permitted the fortification of the town with stone walls and four stone gates. The walls were never built, but a rampart was raised to defend the northeastern approaches. This stretched north from the junction of St Ann Street and St Martin's Church Street, crossed the Green Croft to the present Council House grounds, and then went westwards to link up with the Castle Street Gate. Only the name Rampart Road and mounds in the Council House grounds remind one of the medieval earthwork. Stone gates were erected in Winchester Street and Castle Street, and remained until the eighteenth century. Today the site of the Castle Street gate is clearly marked. It is doubtful whether gates were ever built in Milford Street or St Ann Street. Bars or barriers were erected, not only at the bridges, but across the main streets. The cost of this defensive work was met by a compulsory levy on all Salisbury citizens, authorized by Parliament in 1388. The Close made provision for its own defence about 1328, for more serious than the threat of attack from without were elements of unrest that were appearing within the city. There were signs of a cleavage between the authority of the Church, where its exercise concerned things temporal, and the material interests of the citizens.

Trouble first occurred as early as 1281 when a thief, William of Dunstable, sought sanctuary in the cathedral. Certain of the townsfolk tried to drag him out, but the cathedral body succeeded in barring their way. A very much more serious clash occurred in 1302 when the citizens refused to pay the aid demanded of them by Bishop Simon of Ghent, who had been called upon to pay tallage to the King. Under the charter of 1227 the bishop had a perfect right to levy the tax, but the citizens appealed to the Crown against it. The verdict they received was an interesting one. They could choose—no liability to tax, then no privileges and responsibilities which had also been theirs under the charter. If they wished to retain the liberties and rights that they had gained since 1227 then they must pay. On 6 April 1305 the Mayor, Richard Ludgershall, and the whole council surrendered the mayoralty and all their exemptions and privileges as free citizens. What followed was a potent illustration of the folly of cutting off a nose to spite a face. Salisbury's trade declined, wealth vanished. Wilton began to take heart again. The unhappy citizens appealed to the Bishop for a restoration of their former state, and on 20 August 1306 an agreement was reached. Its preamble gives contemporary opinion, biased admittedly, on the favoured position of Salisbury's sons. 'Our reverend mother, the Church of Sarum, nourished and raised up the children whom she had trans/ ferred . . . unto the spacious fields of pleasantness. Thither she had gathered them as a hen gathereth her chickens, procuring from the illustrious Prince Henry the Third, that the place should be a free and pleasant city, and its sons endowed with manifold prerogatives. They were indeed so strengthened with privileges, that fame publicly pro/ claimed these citizens a chosen race, and the city itself so glorious in many respects that he deemed himself happy who was considered worthy to become a citizen, and to share in its liabilities and exemptions.'

Under the terms of the new agreement the controlling power of the Bishop and the civic responsibilities of the citizens were more clearly defined. A new charter was granted by Edward I (1306) to take the place of the one that had been abrogated.

But the elements of unrest continued, and were accentuated in the difficult years of Edward II's reign and of Edward III's minority. Bishop Simon of Ghent threatened with excommunication those who injured the persons of ecclesiastics and invaded church property. Dean and canons appealed for protection to his successor, Bishop Roger de Mortival. He obtained leave to build a stone wall with battlements about the Close but he died before the work was started. In 1327 Edward III granted the Dean and Chapter licence to surround the Close with an 'embattled wall of stone, and to hold it so enclosed to themselves and their successors, without let or hindrance from himself, his heirs, or their ministers and officers'.

That wall, with its splendid gates, still stands, forming, as it were, a casket for one of the most precious of England's jewels—for such, indeed, is Salisbury Close. The great wall surrounding the old palace of the bishops has been mellowed by the years, and is more suggestive of tales of chivalry and romance than of fortified defence. On the north side of the Close the wall is hidden at the back of gardens, but it is there, stretching westward to the river. The gates, except for their pointed arches, differ in design; the High Street Gate (Pl. 12), once equipped with a portcullis as an additional defence against the town, being the most elaborate. Today, as through the centuries, the gates are shut nightly, and at such other times as the well-being of the Close demands. The stone for all this mural building came, by royal permission, from the demolition of the old cathedral on the hill. Many of the stones are sculptured. In all probability they had been carved by the masons of the great Roger who enriched Old Sarum's Norman cathedral. Close walls and gates proved their value during the episcopate of Robert Wyvil, for the citizens were so antagon- istic to the bishop that Edward III imposed a fine of three thousand marks on them, a fine which they escaped paying by complete submission to the Bishop, who interceded with the King on their behalf.

Reference has already been made to the interest in and generosity to the cathedral and city of New Sarum shown by Henry III, Edward I, and Edward III. In the long line of rulers from 1220 to 1547 there seem to be only two—Edward II and the boy-king Edward V—who did not visit the town. The proximity of the royal palace of Clarendon, only two and a half miles away, partly accounts for the frequency of Court visits to Salisbury, though many royal visitors preferred the hospitality of the bishop's palace. Another reason for its popularity lies in the fact that this new, comparatively clean and healthy town provided a safe and pleasant resort during the outbreaks of plague that were all too common in medieval England. Not that Salisbury always escaped disaster. It had frequent floods. It suffered severely when the Black Death ravaged the whole country in 1348, and again from plague in 1477.

The coming and going of kings brought the city into touch with events of national importance. In 1289 Edward I met in Salisbury the Com- missioners appointed to arrange a marriage between his son and Princess Margaret of Scotland: a match that would have united the crowns of England and Scotland in 1307, had not the untimely death of the little 'maid of Norway' prevented it. In 1297 Edward was in Salisbury again, this time to meet the barons. He ordered them to lead their forces overseas against Gascony. The Constable, the Earl of Hereford, opposed the

command. 'By God, Sir Earl', cried the angry king, 'you will either go
or hang.' 'By God, Sir King', replied the Constable, 'I will neither go
nor hang.' Nor did he. In Edward II's reign two Salisbury bishops,
Simon of Ghent and Roger de Mortival, opposed the King's evil rule.
Counting on local support, the wretched Mortimer who, with the
infamous Queen Isabella, seized power during Edward III's minority,
summoned, quite illegally, a Parliament to meet in Salisbury. 'He
[Mortimer] came, and others of his covyne, with force and arms. When
the prelates were assembled to consult on the affairs of the King, he broke
open the doors and threatened them with loss of life and limb if they
should arrive at anything contrary to his will.' He received no support and
his overthrow came quickly.

Edward III was a good friend to Salisbury, adding to the wealth of the
citizens by his wise regulations for trade, but, at the same time, strengthening the hands of episcopal authority. Under Richard II, however,
Salisbury felt the weight of royal displeasure. The Black Death had
created much local unrest, and many citizens sympathized with Wat
Tyler's rebellion in 1381. Consequently the Mayor and other members of
the commune were summoned to London, charged with being guilty of
'divers enormous violences and trespasses'. They were told that any further
disobedience towards the King, or his Council, or the Bishop, would be
punished by a crippling fine.

Salisbury men did not forget this. Nor could they stomach Richard's
extravagance and neglect of trade. Henry Bolingbroke found staunch
supporters among them, and after Richard's deposition the new king sent
a grateful letter to the city: 'We greatly thank you, and will always regard
you favourably, knowing this that you have a good will to be loyal to us
and truly obedient. We intend and purpose to be a good lord and friend
to you, and to preserve your liberties and franchises.' This the citizens
must have regarded as highly encouraging and they made great preparations to welcome Henry IV when he visited Salisbury in 1404. Every
royal visit was the occasion for a new supply of robes for members of the
commune, different colours—scarlet, crimson, or green—being chosen to
mark the differing dignity of the wearers. Woe betide any citizen who
arrayed himself in a colour to which he was not entitled. One, Henry
Southwyk, was fined forty shillings in 1412 for daring so to do.

The reign of Henry V saw the city full of martial activity. The Bishop,
as a feudal vassal, had to raise men, fitly accoutred, and supplies for the
French war. Levies from elsewhere passed through the town, or were
lodged for a night near by, on their way to Southampton. In 1414 there
was an affray on Fisherton Bridge between the citizens and a party of
soldiers wearing the Earl of Leicester's badge. Three Salisbury men were
killed. The mayoral accounts for that year show a payment 'to a minstrel
of Wales for making him a hood, because he lost his hood in defence of
the City, in the insult offered on the bridge at Fisherton by the men of the

1. View of Old Sarum from the south. Water-colour by Constable.

2. Aerial view of Old Sarum. The site of the cathedral is dominated by the castle.

3. The south wing of de Vaux College, founded about 1260, now de Vaux Lodge. From a water colour by Miss Benson, *c.* 1830, in Salisbury Museum.

4. De Vaux House with Harnham Gate in the distance. The house incorporates part of the east wing of the college.

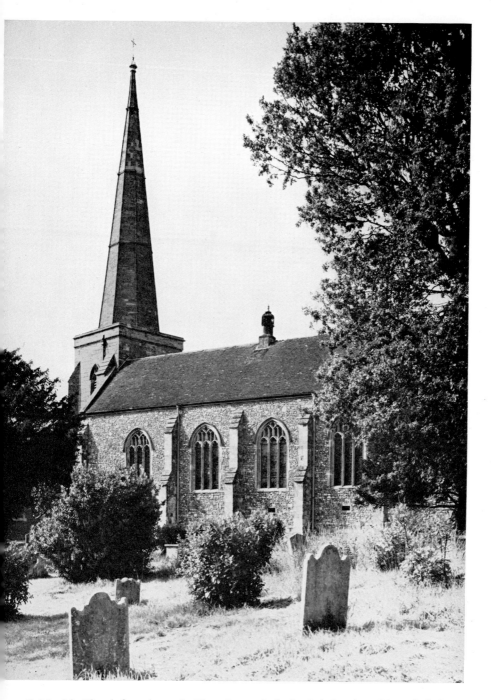

5. St Martin's Church from the south. The spire was built shortly before that of the cathedral.

6. The Joiners' Hall. A fine Jacobean façade in St Ann Street.

7. The Doom over the chancel arch in St Thomas's Church. The painting was uncovered in 1819 and later drastically restored.

8. Castle Street looking south, with the remains of the city gate on the left.

9. The Swayne Chapel in St Thomas's Church. The moulded and decorated roof and murals are all fifteenth century.

10. The Chapel of Trinity Hospital. Rebuilt early in the eighteenth century.

12. The High Street from the north gate of the Close. The statue is of Edward VII.

11. Minster Street looking south. An early nineteenth-century print showing a canal, and the half-timbered buildings which

13. Bishop Jewel's *Apology* chained to the lectern in Great Durnford Church. Behind is an owl capital of the twelfth-century chancel arch.

14. Sir Richard Grobham's tomb in the chancel of Great Wishford Church. A witness to the riches of the Spanish galleon awarded to his master Sir Thomas Gorges.

15. Longford Castle from the formal garden. Part of the Elizabethan building.

16. The seventeenth-century south front of Wilton House, designed by Inigo Jones and Webb. The Tudor tower in the middle of the east side was a part of the original house.

18. The Hertford monument in the cathedral. Recalling the tragic story of Lady Catherine Grey and her husband Edward Seymour, later Earl of Hertford, and their two sons born in the Tower.

17. The Gorges monument in the cathedral. A curious composition of scientific and classical forms. The stained-glass window is a memorial to George Herbert.

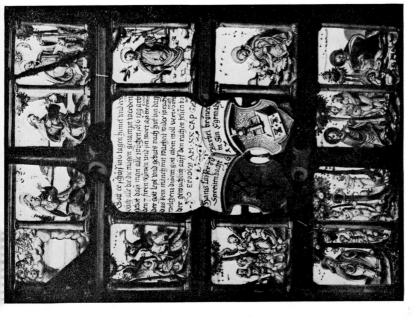

20. Small seventeenth-century Swiss glazed panel in St Edmund's Church. Like the window of this church destroyed by Henry Sherfield in 1629 it depicts the story of the Creation.

19. Elihonor Sadler's monument in the south aisle of the cathedral.

21. The Pheasant Inn in Salt Lane. From the seventeenth century a room at the back of this inn was used as the Shoemakers' Hall.

22. St John Street looking north. St Ann's Gate and Malmesbury House are on the left, with the King's Arms opposite.

23. St Edmund's Church. The tower was rebuilt in 1653 after the original nave was destroyed.

24. The College of Matrons in the Close. Founded by Bishop Seth Ward for the widows of Salisbury and Exeter clergy.

25. The King's House in the Close. Formerly the prebendal house of the Abbots of Sherborne. was much enlarged by Thomas Sadler early in the seventeenth century.

Earl of Leicester'. On 11 August 1415 Henry V arrived at Salisbury with his army. He camped outside the city, on the slopes of Bishop's Down and Laverstock. The following day the march to Southampton was resumed, with a contingent of Salisbury men following the royal banner. An official account of the Agincourt campaign, written in old French, is still preserved in the municipal archives. In the reign of Henry VI Salisbury played a part in the naval operations of the Hundred Years War. Since the Avon was a navigable river from Christchurch to Salisbury until the reign of Queen Elizabeth, the city was technically a seaport. As such it built and manned a ship—the *Trout*—which helped in the defence of the Kent coast.

Wars and rumours of wars seem to have enhanced rather than to have diminished Salisbury's prosperity. The first half of the fifteenth century was its heyday. Men in authority needed money to meet the exigencies of the times, and the citizens learnt that their fat purses gave them a powerful means of bargaining for their own advantage. There was a restless, rebellious spirit abroad. Some Salisbury men went so far as to support Jack Cade's rising, and it was a Salisbury butcher who murdered Bishop Ayscough at Edington—a crime for which the city was compelled to exhibit one of the unhappy Cade's quarters. Others adopted more Machiavellian tactics to gain their ends, under the leadership of John Halle and John a'Porte.

Early in Edward IV's reign, Bishop Beauchamp granted to William Swayne a small piece of land near St Thomas's Church. Swayne pur, posed to build there a stone house for the priest who served the chantry chapel of the Tailors' Guild. John Halle, then Mayor, seems to have hated Swayne with all the force of his arrogant, overbearing nature. He stated that the land in question belonged to the Mayor and Corporation of Salisbury, and promptly carried the matter to the highest authority by an appeal to the King. The Bishop, he said, had acted out of 'pure malice' and described his action as likely to endanger the lives and prosperity of the King's 'poor and true liegemen'. With every outward sign of respect, Halle next presented the Bishop with the request that he should relinquish not only the piece of land in dispute but also all his feudal rights over the city, in return for a fee-farm rent which would give him in exchange a good annual sum. The Bishop indignantly refused even to consider such a request, and immediately sent his own account of events to the King, relating how Halle had incited a number of men to demolish the half-built house at St Thomas's.

There was, of course, much more at stake than the priest's dwelling, which was eventually built and is today used as a vestry. The old order of established authority was at loggerheads with a new power based on wealth. Halle was summoned to London, where he behaved with such effrontery in Edward's presence that he was committed to prison. Salisbury received a royal command to choose another mayor. This it refused to do.

E

The King expressed his great displeasure at the citizens' obduracy, and ordered them to elect another mayor forthwith or to send a number of representatives to London, there to answer at the palace of Westminster for the city's disobedience. The citizens refused to elect another mayor, and set about the business of appointing a delegation. Their first choice was John Halle, who was still in prison. The others, John a'Porte among them, went to Westminster, where the King refused to discuss matters with a body whose principal member, then in gaol, was the chief cause of all the trouble. Weeks of delay in London, with its heavy expenses, added to the probable losses that were befalling their businesses at home, brought the delegation to its senses. On the receipt of an urgent request from John a'Porte, Salisbury elected John Chafyn as mayor, and the delegation returned home without ever seeing the King.

Yet when Edward IV visited Salisbury soon afterwards he was splendidly entertained by the Mayor, John Halle! Trouble between the Bishop and citizens was by no means over. Halle became more docile with old age, but John a'Porte refused to take the customary mayoral oath to the Bishop and was as defiant as his predecessor, though less noisy. Episcopal appeals to the Crown were rendered ineffectual by a renewal of the Wars of the Roses. It was not until Whitsun 1474 that the struggle between the Bishop and the citizens ended, apparently in the complete victory of the Bishop, to whom was sent an abject plea for pardon. 'We submit us', said the citizens, 'in every and all matters . . . beseeching his good grace that of his fatherly pity he would conserve his said citizens and city in reasonable privilege.' The restitution of the *status quo* was only apparent, for the death knell of the feudal organization of society had already sounded throughout the country. During the years of internal struggle, important in the city's growth as a municipality, seeds had been sown and carried on more than local winds. They took root in the deeply disturbed soil of English social life and came to harvest within two generations. Their fruits can be seen in the civic and religious organization of modern Salisbury.

With the accession of the Tudors medievalism moved rapidly to its close. For a brief space the city had peace, law, and order under Henry VII, and enjoyed, as never before, its opportunities for pageantry, merrymaking, and feasting. It almost seemed as if men were cognizant of the imminence of change and wished to make the most of the old order while it lasted. The festivals and Holy Days of the Church, and the feasts and processions of the trade guilds, were observed with increasing splendour. By the fifteenth century thirty-four of Salisbury's industries had been organized into nineteen guilds, and during the summer months every week contained annual feast-days of one or other of them. The Confraternity of the Tailors' Guild provided in 1496, when Henry VII visited the city, the giant figure of St Christopher, still to be seen in the Museum and still paraded through the streets on great occasions. What a gorgeous cavalcade must have welcomed Henry Tudor! It was decreed that 'all the twenty-four who have been mayors shall ride in scarlet to meet the king, all not mayors shall ride in crimson, and the forty-eight in green'. Trade was good, food and drink were plentiful, and the town gave itself whole-heartedly to the festivities it loved, with minstrels, mummers, dancers, bear-leaders, wrestlers, and jugglers to provide entertainment for the crowds.

The city's Whitsun Fair, held for centuries within the precincts of the Close, was associated not only with trade and merry-making but also with the performance of morality plays for which a guild, or a group of guilds, would undertake the responsibility for a scene. May Day was another festal occasion. It was celebrated with feasting and morris dancing, and it was for the latter that the city's Hob Nob (the local name for Hobby Horse) was first devised. But there were two anniversaries which particularly aroused the excitement and enthusiasm of the citizens. One was St George's Day, 23 April, when the streets of Salisbury saw the 'Riding of the George', the great procession headed by the Guild of St George (the Mayor and the members of the two councils) and followed by representatives of the guilds and other inhabitants summoned to attend. Richly clad, with minstrels playing and banners flying, they rode to attend Mass in the Chapel of St George in St Thomas's Church, and then returned to the Guild Hall for the appropriate banquet. It was essentially the festival of the town. The other anniversary—and this was the supreme red-letter day for Salisbury—was St Osmund's Day. Although St Osmund had not been canonized until 1457 he had been honoured as the patron saint of the new city since its beginning, and his shrine in the cathedral, whither his body had been removed from Old Sarum in 1226, was associated with many miracles and held in great veneration. In the Church Calendar his commemoration falls on 4 December, but Salisbury kept his day, for practical reasons, in mid-summer on 16 July.[1] It was a general holiday, with processions, pageants, and feasting that continued far into the night, when the darkness was dispelled by the light of innumerable torches. So great was the feasting, so deep the potations, that the authorities saw to it that clubs were available with which strong men could reinforce the efforts of the constables to maintain order. Observed very differently was the Eve of St Osmund. This was kept as a Wake or Solemn Watch, when 'for the honour of the city', the members of every craft, men and women, attired themselves 'in the best manner that may be', and at seven o'clock in the evening attended upon the Mayor in the Market Place to follow him silently to the saint's shrine in the cathedral, there to keep vigil.

Medieval Salisbury had been created by the inspiration and genius of her bishops, and the energy and enterprise of her citizens. When, in the sixteenth century, the power of the state intervened, the character of the

[1] The date of St Osmund's burial in the Cathedrad.

city changed. Students of de Vaux, Franciscan and Dominican friars, secular canons from St Edmund's, were seen no more in her streets. Shrines were demolished, chantry chapels, centres of worship for the guilds, ceased to exist. No longer could the Tailors go on the Eve of Midsummer to the Chapel of St John on the bridge. The 'Riding of the George' faded into a memory. There was no patron saint. In July 1545 came a resolution of the corporation: 'It is agreed that the Watche on St Osmund's night be noe more observed or kepte.' With that decree the medieval history of the cathedral city of Salisbury came to an end.

The names of the great men who inspired and directed the building and development of medieval Salisbury are known and honoured, but their work would have been impossible without the help and labour of ordinary men and women. Only a rough estimate can be made of the growth of the population between 1220 and 1545. John Ivie, Mayor in 1627, gave a hint when he wrote that the Great Plague reduced the city's numbers to three thousand—probably about half the population of a year earlier. Judging from this, there may have been as many as five thousand people in Salisbury in 1545. If this figure is anywhere near correct it shows a marked increase in the course of three hundred years, for in 1220, according to tradition, only one hundred men and women came down from the hill with Bishop Poore. A rapid rise of population during the Middle Ages would have been checked by the heavy death-roll of the Black Death, the shortness of the medieval span of life, and terribly high infant mortality. Most of Salisbury's inhabitants worked with their hands as craftsmen: a comparative few were master merchants: there were traders of many kinds, innkeepers, ostlers, packmen, cooks, servants, and labourers engaged in meeting the needs of everyday life. Living celibate lives in canonical houses, priests' lodgings, and halls, were clergy, friars, and scholars. It was a mixed community, containing widely differing degrees of wealth and poverty: of actual beggary there would have been little in a time of full employment.

The city was feudal in that it was subject to its overlord, the Bishop, but the feudalism which limited personal freedom and mobility was already in its death-throes when Salisbury was founded, and expired completely before 1545. Only for the children of the poorer classes did a condition resembling serfdom exist, for with the industrial revolution of the thirteenth century they were put to work at a very early age. For the rest of the population the standard of living steadily rose. Medieval dress, like medieval architecture, became increasingly decorative and colourful, and, while humble folk clung to hooded tunics and leather jerkins, rich citizens added collars of fur and linings of silk to their 'comely gowns' of good cloth, and their wives copied the fashions of the great ladies who visited Salisbury. An indication of the city's prosperity is given by the fact that almost all its people 'walked on leather': very few went barefoot, and clogs were practically unknown.

Sufficient fifteenth-century domestic building survives in Salisbury to show that the houses of the well-to-do became much more comfortable and commodious. They were better equipped, too, and meals became much more pleasant when such refinements as spoons and forks—often of silver—were adopted. The clay and wattle houses still in use must have deteriorated over the years into hovels and breeding grounds of disease. Cleanliness, even in a place as plentifully supplied with water as Salisbury, left much to be desired, and the practice of covering floors with rushes—often unmoved for a year—and of sharing the living room, often the only room, with dogs, produced an abundance of fleas. It is not surprising that visitations of plague became more frequent towards the end of the medieval period. As far as food was concerned the people did well, and the tables of the wealthy were heavily laden at the customary two meals a day. Fish, cheese, butter, bread, ale, and honey were plentiful. The meat was mainly beef and pork, sheep being valued more for the production of wool than of mutton. Oxen were slaughtered for their hides as well as for their meat. In the 'blood month' of October all superfluous cattle were killed, and the tanners replenished their stocks of leather and the butchers salted down meat for winter consumption. Generally speaking, the pattern of life in Salisbury differed little from that of other medieval towns made prosperous by the wool trade.

It was a close-knit, interdependent society bound together in common loyalty to the Church and, nominally at any rate, in duty to the Bishop. When these ties broke, the Middle Ages were over and the city started on a new phase of its history, but by that time visions had been turned into realities, plans into accomplished facts. To this fulfilment the lives, work, and wealth of the men and women of medieval Salisbury contributed. All unknowingly, they provided the life-blood which gave the city its vitality and strength. In the twentieth century she holds their dust and is the guardian of all that still exists of their creation. It is their great memorial.

III

REFORMATION IN SALISBURY

1535–1660

I

THE PERIOD from the end of the Middle Ages and the start of the Reformation in 1535, until the Restoration in 1660, marks one of the stormiest transitions in English history. In Salisbury it made a lasting imprint. In religion, the change was from Romanism to Reform, back to Romanism, then to Puritanism, and finally to the settled Church of England; in politics, from Tudor and Stuart despotism through all the horrors of the Civil War to the Commonwealth and the beginnings of constitutional monarchy; in civic affairs it saw the growth of the powerful trade guilds and the final victory of the city over the bishop; in the surrounding countryside the fall of the monasteries paved the way for the rise of the great country houses with their incalculable influence on art and literature; finally, in architecture the change was from the Gothic to the Classical by way of the exquisite Renaissance building of the Tudors.

At the dissolution of the monasteries, Salisbury, being a cathedral of secular canons, suffered comparatively little except in the grievous loss and destruction of its treasures, chief among them the shrine of St Osmund. Its chantries, however, were dissolved and their funds taken, and in the city the only remaining religious foundation was the Hospital of St Nicholas. Even the Grey and Black Friars, poor as they were, suffered the common fate, and their churches and buildings were destroyed for the sake of the materials. The House of the Scholars of de Vaux was spared for a few years but was dissolved in 1543, not because it was educational, but because much of its property had been given to pay for prayers for benefactors, and so it came under the Chantry Act. The actual building and some of its property, including the manors of East and West Harnham, were granted to Sir Michael Lister. Similarly, in 1546 St Edmund's College was granted to William St Barbe, a gentleman of the King's Privy Chamber, for £400, and, although a layman, he became Provost and Rector of St Edmund's Church with the proviso 'That divine service and the cure of souls were not neglected'.

Of the fifteen religious houses in Wiltshire, with their 175 inmates and a total revenue of £4,184, we are only here concerned with the nunneries of Amesbury and Wilton. Amesbury, which had been given by Henry II to the great abbey of Fontevrault in Anjou, was surrendered on 4 December 1539 and its annual income of £553 annexed by the King, who granted it two years later to his brother-in-law, Sir Edward Seymour, later Lord Protector Somerset, whose son Edward, Earl of Hertford, married Lady Catherine Grey.

Wilton, with its income of £652, had been surrendered nine months earlier. The last abbess of this great Saxon foundation, Cecily Bodenham, had written personally to Thomas Cromwell, asking for some relief from the ruling of the King's special visitor Doctor Legh, who had confined not only all the sisters but herself to the house. She did not mind this for her own part but wrote that

> in consideration of thadmynystracion of myne office and specially of this poore house which is in greate debte and requirith moche reparacon and also whiche wt oute good husbandry is not like in long season to come forwarde . . . yt maye pleas yor Mr ship of yor goodness to licence me being associate with oon or two of the sad and discrete Sisters of my house to supervise abrode suche thinges as shalbe for the prouffitte & commoditie of my house which thing though peradventure myght bee done by other, yet I ensure you that none will doo hit soo faithfully for my house prouffitte as myne owne selfe.

She promised not to be away at night unless by 'inevitable necessitie' she could not return home, and also asked permission that if any of her Sisters were visited by their near relatives they 'maye have licence to speke wt them in the hall in my presens or my prioresse & other two discrete Sisters'. The abbey and all its great possessions was granted in 1542 to Sir William Herbert, created Earl of Pembroke in 1551.

Nothing could have been more disastrous than the frequent changes of authority in religious matters at this period. Within the space of ten years England was ruled by Henry VIII, who had overthrown Roman authority but still clung to the Mass and Roman doctrine; by Edward VI and that ardent Protestant, his uncle Somerset; by Mary with a complete return to Romanism; and by Elizabeth, who with her genius for statecraft, achieved a working compromise. That most versatile of bishops, John Salcot, *alias* Capon, performed a *tour de force* at Salisbury by squaring his conscience with all these changes—except the last, and that only because he died in 1557. He also enriched himself at the expense of his see so that John Jewel, succeeding him in 1560 after a three-year vacancy, said that 'a capon has devoured all'. During Salcot's episcopate many terrible scenes were enacted in Salisbury, when martyrs for the Protestant faith were burned at the stake. Most famous of these was John Maundrel, unworthily commemorated in recent times by the Maundrel Hall in Fisherton Street, since converted into a showroom for furniture.

A husbandman himself, Maundrel was the son of a farmer at Rowde, but lived with his wife and children in the parish of Keevil. Unable to read, he carried the New Testament about him so that it could always be read to him, and such was his memory that he could recite most of it by heart: Foxe adds 'his conversation and living being very honest and charitable as his neighbours are able to testifie'. We see him first in the market-place at Devizes, arrayed in a white sheet and carrying a candle for having spoken against holy water and bread at Edington Abbey. Later he decided, with John Spicer, a freemason, and William Coberly, a tailor, to go to Keevil parish church, where the three of them made a demonstration against 'idols' during a procession. All three by order of the vicar were put in the stocks, then brought before a Justice of the Peace and the next day sent to Salisbury, where they were taken before Bishop Capon and Geffrey, Chancellor of the Diocese. Imprisonment followed. Finally they were examined in Fisherton Anger church (which was pulled down in 1852) and asked to state their beliefs. They affirmed their faith in the creed and in the scriptures 'from the first of Genesis to the last of the Apocalypse' but refused to subscribe to the Living Presence or to the Pope's authority, saying that 'the Popish Masse was abominable Idolatrie'. Maundrel with reckless courage added 'that wooden Images were good to rost a shoulder of mutton, but evill in the Church'.

The Chancellor condemned them and delivered them to the Sheriff on 23 March 1555, and next day 'they were carried out of the common Goale to a place betwixt Salisburie and Wilton, where were two postes set for them to be burnt at. Which men comming [sic] to the place, they kneeled down and made their prayers secretly together, and then being disclothed to their shirts, John Maundrel spake with a loud voice, Not for all Salisbury, which words men judged to be an answer to the Sheriff, which offered the Queene's pardon if he would recant, And after that in like manner spake John Spicer, saying, This is the joyfullest day that ever I saw. Thus were they 3 burnt at two stakes where most constantly they gave their bodies to the fire, and their soules to the Lord for testimonie of his Truth.'

Two other men, John Hunt and Richard White, both husbandmen of Marlborough, were more fortunate. Although they were condemned to death by Dr Geffrey, Mr Michel (the under-Sheriff of Wiltshire), instead of burning them, burned the writ, and before it could be renewed both Geffrey and Queen Mary were dead.

So many innocent people were executed in those days, either for their religious beliefs or because they stood too close to the Crown, that it almost comes as a relief to hear of a real criminal being brought to justice. The fanatical Charles, Lord Stourton, was hanged with a silken rope in Salisbury market-place in 1556 for the murder, in treacherous and revolting circumstances, of a father and son named Hartgill. After persecuting them for years, besieging them in their house, and getting them imprisoned in the Fleet, Stourton decoyed them to a meeting on their release and had them bound and carried to his house. There, on a terrace, they were done to death by his people, while Lord Stourton looked on from a doorway.

Bishop Jewel found a state of utter chaos in the diocese of Salisbury, but in the eleven years for which he held the See he brought about a transformation. Salisbury, however, bears him a grudge for the destruction in her cathedral and parish churches of 'idolatrous' stained-glass windows, most of which perished after his decree of 1567. The patron of poor scholars, he befriended Richard Hooker, sending him to Corpus Christi College, Oxford, and it was at Boscombe Vicarage near Salisbury that Hooker wrote the first four books of his *Ecclesiastical Polity*. Jewel's own great work, the *Apology for the Church of England*, was ordered by Queen Elizabeth to be chained to the desk in every parish church in England, and is still to be seen at Great Durnford in the Avon Valley (Pl. 13). Constantly he visited every part of his large diocese, preaching to the people and cleaning up abuses, until, worn out with sickness and overwork, he died on a preaching tour in September 1571, at the early age of forty-nine.

A new chapter in the struggle between the two forms of religious belief began in 1578, when the Privy Council issued the decrees against recusancy and it became a crime not to go to church, or to be 'hynderers or contemnors of the Religion sett forth by her Majestie', or to be in possession of mass books. In the Salisbury area Lord Arundell of War-dour and Mr Webb of Odstock were penalized under this decree, and at the Summer Assize in 1583 at New Sarum, Richard Cable of White-parish, yeoman, was allowed bail for £200 and had to appear at the next sessions when he would either forfeit £80 'for his refusal to go to church' or 'surrender . . . his body to prison'.

Not only were the remaining chantries seized under the Act of 1547, but the Commissioners were empowered to take and sell the possessions of the chantries and chapels of the City Guilds and fraternities. In St Thomas's church, where the great merchant guild of St George had its chapel, the churchwardens' accounts show that 'the George' was taken down by carpenters and labourers, new glass was put in the windows to replace coloured glass, the brasses, weighing two hundredweight, sold for 36s., and the 'footstools of the images in the church' broken down. It cost 3s. 6d. 'to make clean the church after the departure of the visitors'. After this the ceremony of choosing the mayor was transferred from St Thomas's to St Edmund's church although in 1579 the plague was so bad in the streets adjoining the latter that it once more took place at St Thomas's. The Guild of Weavers and the Guild of Tailors were rich enough to buy back their revenues and estates apart from those connected with their chantries and chapels. During Elizabeth's reign many of the old trade guilds began to form themselves into companies as their wealth and power increased. As we have seen, much of the old pageantry disappeared at the time of the Reformation and the 'Riding of the George' on 23 April with St Osmund's night on 15 July became remembered splendours only. The powerful Tailors' Guild, however, retained their Midsummer Feast and pageant, and in 1570 'the Gyant, the thre black boyes, the bearer of the gyant, and one person to playe the Divell's part' appeared as usual with the customary morris dancers bedecked with bells, and amongst the inventory that year we find 'one Hobby-Horse, and one mayde Marrian's Coate with a kertell, and a gyrdell of red crimson sarcent, and a Cloke and a vellet cappe'.

Along with wealth and splendour went poverty and squalor. Some praiseworthy attempts were made to deal with the condition of the streets, and the picturesque if insanitary rivulets that flowed through most of them. In 1562 Anthony Weekes, at a salary of £20 a year, agreed to find a scavenger cart and carry out of the city 'for as many as do paye watche and warde, all suche myre, durt, dust and soyle' as lay in the streets, especially on Wednesdays and Saturdays, always provided they were not 'hollydayes'. The citizens were bound to make tidy heaps of their refuse to facilitate the work but were not allowed to include stable dung or garden weeds. In 1578 those living on the town ditch were taxed for its upkeep and cleanliness.

The city fathers took their duties seriously, and we get an interesting comparison with modern methods when we read that in 1595 the 'XLVIIJ of this Cittie' were ordered to divide themselves into three companies in order to make a survey of all the houses in the city. 'And where they shall finde any houses oppressed with more tenants or in-habitantes than are to be thought convenient in respect of the houses, to give them warninge foorthwith to provide themselves elsewheres.' Over-crowding was 'to incurre suche punishment and paine as shalbe inflicted on them'.

The new Council House, first decided on in December 1565, was not begun until 1579 nor finished until 1584. Possibly 'the Forty-eight' had been influenced by the fact that in June 1565 four citizens had overheard Bishop Jewel say that 'the Maior of Sarum was his maiour and the people of Sarum his subjectes'. Bishop Coldwell in 1593 repeated the affront by referring to the Mayor in a document as 'absolutely his Maior'; after a protest the claim was withdrawn, but another quarrel ensued, with the Mayor refusing to take the oath and both sides appealing, without definite result, both to Queen Elizabeth and the Lord Chief Justice. It was not until the next reign that the city was to gain the independence for which it had fought so long.

In the surrounding countryside three great houses were now rising to fame. Longford Castle (Pl. 15), unlike the other two, owed nothing to the fall of the monasteries but was built on the site of an old manor house. It is a romantic story, closely interwoven with the history of the period.

One of Queen Elizabeth's most persistent suitors was Eric, son of King Gustavus I of Sweden. In 1559 the King came to England himself and stayed with William Parr, Marquess of Northampton, brother of Queen Catherine Parr, Henry VIII's widow. In 1560 Eric came to the throne and, his brother John having failed as an ambassador, in 1564 sent his sister Cecilia, Margravine of Baden, to plead his cause. With her, as one of her suite, came a beautiful girl of fifteen, Helena Snachenberg, daughter of a Swedish nobleman. It was a terrible journey. Owing to trouble between Sweden and Denmark, the party first travelled four hundred miles by water to Finland, and then seven hundred miles over ice right across the coast of northern Europe in mid-winter, until they eventually came to Calais, whence, after long delay, they reached Dover. Four days after her arrival in London, the Princess gave birth to a child. Helena Snachenberg never faced the journey again, and remained in England until her death, seventy years later.

Queen Elizabeth, fascinated by the girl, made her a Maid of Honour and she soon became 'Chief Lady of the Privy Chamber'. The Marquess of Northampton fell in love with her and married her seven months after her arrival, before she was sixteen. The Queen was present at the wedding, but only five years later had the sad task of paying for the Marquess's funeral expenses. The young Marchioness remained a widow nine years and then married Sir Thomas Gorges, member of an ancient Wiltshire family of Norman extraction.

Together they built Longford Castle, the plans for which were once thought to have been prepared by John Thorpe, and it is said that it was by the wish of the Marchioness (as she continued to be called) that it was built in triangular form to symbolize the Holy Trinity. It took thirteen years to build, and proved so costly that Helena begged for the hull of a Spanish treasure galleon, wrecked at the time of the Armada, from the Queen, which not only relieved her husband's immediate difficulties but made him and his steward, Sir Richard Grobham, rich men for life. The latter's splendid tomb in Wishford church bears testimony to his wealth (Pl. 14).

In Sidney's *Arcadia*, Longford is the 'Castle of Amphialeus', and Spenser, in 'Colin Clout's come home again', is referring to the Lady Helena as Mansilia in the passage that runs:

> *No less praiseworthy is Mansilia*
> *Best known by bearing up great Cynthia's train . . .*
> *She is the paterne of true womanhead*
> *And only mirrhor of feminitie;*
> *Worthy next after Cynthia to tread,*
> *As she is next to her in nobilitie.*

At Elizabeth's funeral the Marchioness was indeed chief mourner, being looked upon as the second lady in the land. At her own death at the age of eighty-six, in 1635, she was found to have left £500 to be laid out in 'blackes' for her household staff. She left ninety-eight descendants. Sir Thomas Gorges and his Marchioness are commemorated in Salisbury Cathedral by the huge monument with their effigies at the east end of the north aisle (Pl. 17).

Balancing this monument, at the same end of the south aisle, is the great tomb of the Hertfords (Pl. 18). Here lie buried Edward, Earl of Hertford, son of Lord Protector Somerset, and his first wife, Lady Catherine Grey, sister of the ill-fated Lady Jane. Catherine had been married as a child of thirteen to Henry Herbert, second son of the first Earl of Pembroke by his wife Anne Parr, sister of Queen Catherine Parr and the Marquess of North-ampton, but on the execution of Lady Jane and her father, the Duke of Suffolk, the prudent Earl got his son to divorce her and send her home.

When Elizabeth succeeded Mary, she was, unlike her sister, consistently unkind to Lady Catherine at Court. The reason undoubtedly was that Lady Catherine, as granddaughter of Henry VIII's sister, Mary Brandon, Duchess of Suffolk, stood next in succession to the throne (after her mother, Frances Grey) under Henry's will. The unkindness changed to rage when Catherine and Edward Seymour fell in love and were secretly married, and the young couple, when this was discovered, were both thrown into the Tower, where shortly afterwards their first son was born. Elizabeth promptly separated them, but through the kindness of warders they were able to meet, and eighteen months later a second son was born. The Queen was still more enraged, and they were kept in close custody and never allowed to meet again. Lady Catherine died of melancholy at the early age of twenty-seven but her husband survived her by over fifty years. The tragic lovers lie in this great tomb, with their sons kneeling beside them. Edward, later Earl of Hertford, lived much at his two estates in Wiltshire, Wulfhall and Amesbury Abbey. As a patron of art and learning, especially of music, he took under his protection William Lawes, brother of Henry, and the brothers, both later to become famous musicians, received their musical education at Amesbury from Coperario, a depen-dant of the Earl. Amesbury Abbey remained in the possession of the Somerset family until 1671: the days of its greatest fame were to be later when Kitty, Duchess of Queensberry, entertained her literary *protégés* there.

On the other hand, Wilton House (Pl. 16), the third of these great houses, reached the height of its literary and social fame at this period. The house was begun, on the site of the Abbey, by Sir William Herbert the year before he became first Earl of Pembroke: according to tradition, Holbein was consulted about the building. No plans are extant, but in the British Museum are several of his architectural drawings, which closely resemble the centre of the east front, which still survives, and the 'Holbein porch', moved by Wyatt into the grounds. It was the marriage in 1577 of Henry the second Earl, to Mary Sidney, as his third wife, which ushered in the glorious years. The sister of Sir Philip Sidney, she was a woman of great learning; her brother spent many years at Wilton, and according to Aubrey:

The Arcadia and Daphne is about Vernditch and Wilton; and those romancy plaines and boscages did, no doubt, conduce to the heightening of Sir Philip Sidney's phansie. He lived much in these parts, and his most masterly touches of his pastoralls he wrote upon the spott where they were conceived.

Not only Sir Philip Sidney, but Edmund Spenser, Philip Massinger, Gerard the herbalist, Ben Jonson, Geoffrey Fenton, the translator of old tales from the French and Italian, Thomas Morley the musician, and Shakespeare himself are all connected with Wilton at this time. Many of them dedicated their works to Mary Sidney, Spenser calling her 'the right noble and beautiful Ladie, the La. Marie, Countesse of Pembroke'. Massinger, son of a dependant of the Earl, was born in Salisbury and baptized in St Thomas's Church on 24 November 1583. Aubrey says he was a servant of Lord Pembroke's and had a pension of £20 or £30 a year. The character of Sir Giles Overreach in *A New Way to Pay Old Debts* was based on that of Sir Giles Mompesson of Bathampton House, Wylye, who was degraded from the order of knighthood, fined £1,000, and, although an M.P., banished in perpetuity by James I for his nefarious financial practices.

'The most Noble and Incomparable pair of Brethren', William, the third Earl, and Philip, the first Earl of Montgomery and later fourth Earl of Pembroke, carried on their mother's tradition, and to them is dedicated by the publishers the first folio of Shakespeare's works. Another dedication to them of a sermon by Walter Sweeper contains these words:

I gained the greatest part of my little learning through my acquaintance with your honourable father's house and family. . . . And your famous Wilton House, like a little Uniuersitie, was a more excellent nurcerie for learning and pietie, than ever it was in former times, when King Edgar's daughter Editha had her residence and regencie there.

Mary Sidney, 'that noble nurse of learning', survived her husband by twenty years; dying in 1621, she was buried in Salisbury Cathedral and there commemorated by the famous lines, perhaps by Ben Jonson, or possibly William Browne:

> Underneath this sable herse
> Lies the subject of all verse,
> Sidney's sister, Pembroke's mother.
> Death, ere thou hast slain another
> Learn'd and fair and good as she,
> Time shall throw a dart at thee.

William, third Earl, succeeded in 1601 at a time when he had been banished from Court by Queen Elizabeth for his love affair with Mary

Fitton, supposed until recently to have been the 'Dark Lady' of Shakespeare's sonnets. There is a tradition that *Twelfth Night* was first acted at
Wilton: *As You Like It* was performed in 1603 when James I was there but,
sad to say, the evidence for the presence of 'the man Shakespeare' on that
occasion is now lost. It was in 1647, during the time of the fourth Earl,
Philip, that the original house, except for the centre of the east front, was
destroyed by fire, and Philip called in Inigo Jones as architect and his
nephew Webb to redesign the interior. It is to Webb that we owe the
magnificent state rooms, including the single and double cube rooms,
with their pine panelling decorated with four or five different shades of
gold leaf and superbly carved wooden swags. Italian artists painted the
ceilings. Philip was the great patron of Van Dyck, who painted the
famous group of the family and many other portraits: his father Henry
had been the patron of antiquaries and heralds and, again according to
Aubrey, 'did set up all the painted glass scutchions about the house'.
These are now mostly in the heads of the windows of Wyatt's plaster
cloisters.

Wilton has always been associated with the entertainment of royalty.
Queen Elizabeth was there in 1573 and both James I and Charles I paid
visits on many occasions: Aubrey indeed states that Charles 'did love
Wilton above all places and came there every summer'. This makes it all
the more strange that early in the Civil War Earl Philip sided with the
Parliamentarians, provoking Samuel Butler, author of *Hudibras*, to
the lampoon which runs:

> *Pembroke's a Covenanting Lord,*
> *That ne'er with God or Man kept word,*
> *One day he'd sware he'd serve the King,*
> *The next was quite another Thing;*
> *Still changing with the Wind and Tide,*
> *That he might keep the stronger Side.*

If Wilton House could entertain royalty, so could the city of Salisbury.
Queen Elizabeth had been there in progress in 1584 when bad weather
spoiled her plan to hunt at Clarendon, and eleven years later 'the Maior
and his bretherne' had the honour of entertaining Don Antonio, King
of Portugal, with his two eldest sons. They were received at the Close
Gate in the High Street and the next night the King and all his company
supped at His Worship's house.

Those were expensive days for Salisbury. It was the city presumably
which provided the golden bell worth 'fyftie poundes and better' in
March 1583 when 'ther was a race runned with horses at the Fursyes, thre
myles from Harnem Hyll', when the Earl of Cumberland, who won it,
promised the Mayor on his honour to bring it again for the next year's
race. 'Also rans' on this first occasion included the Earls of Warwick,
Pembroke, and Essex, the Lords Thomas and William Howard, Sir

Walter Hungerford, Sir John Danvers, Mr Thomas Gorges, and many others. Visiting royalty always expected and received rich gifts. James I at his first visit in 1603 was given a 'cuppe of silver, double gilded and covered . . . of the valewe of Twentie markes . . . and twentie poundes in gould to be putt therein', and at the same time Lord Pembroke was

FIG. 11. Cecil crest at No. 17 The Close

given 'one fatt oxe of the price of eight pounds', presumably to help with his housekeeping. The mace had to be regilt and decorated with the King's arms, the citizens had to illuminate the city during the King's visit by placing lanterns and candles at their doorways, 'the twenty-four' city fathers were ordered to be arrayed in scarlet gowns, 'the forty-eight' in citizens' gowns 'with their horses and footcloths' to accompany the Mayor.

It proved a good investment and paid rich dividends. Even at James's first visit the authorities were trying to obtain a *quid pro quo* by petitioning him to make the city a county and so to be incorporated 'with the trades therein for the prevencion of the decaye thereof'. No stone was left unturned to free it finally from the overlordship of the bishop. Early in 1606 the Mayor and others decided to confer with the Dean and Chapter to obtain their consent to procuring a corporation; they had a friend at Court in the person of Sir Robert Cecil, now Secretary of State and later Earl of Salisbury, who had lived in the Close, and to this day the old crest of the Cecils, a sheaf supported by two lions rampant (Fig. 11), may be seen in the cornice of a room at Number 17. Other petitions to the King followed, about the influx of strangers who ignored the guild rules, and about criminals who evaded the law owing to judiciary powers being administered by the bishop instead of the mayor and justices. Finally, in 1612, the long-awaited charter was granted. Bishop Cotton was allowed to save face by keeping control of the Close and the Mayor had to take the oath in his presence. All the trade companies were reconstituted, and, to quote Haskins, 'no one was allowed to trade in the City unless he had received the freedom of the City and was a member of one of the companies'. The Mayor and Corporation were at last in being with an army of officials to maintain law and order, and the Mayor, to be elected annually, had large powers and responsibilities. The cost of the charter was met by voluntary contributions from all the merchants, traders, and craftsmen of the city.

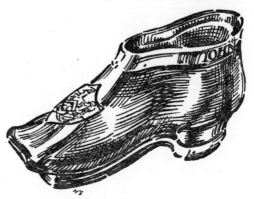

FIG. 12. The Shoemakers' drinking cup

Many of the old guilds now formed themselves into companies, and during the next two decades received their charters of incorporation. It is at this period, too, that several new halls were built; the beautiful Joiners' Hall (Pl. 6) in St Ann Street survives as to its exterior but the minutely carved panelling with Corinthian pillars which decorated the hall (measuring 29 feet by 27 feet) has long since disappeared. The Shoemakers' Hall, bequeathed in 1638 to his father's company by Philip Crewe, a schoolmaster, is now a part of the Pheasant Inn (Pl. 21); the fine oak panelling from the original Weavers' Hall in Endless Street now adorns the premises of the London and Liverpool Insurance Company at the corner of Queen Street and Winchester Street, while many of the coats of arms and other relics belonging to the trade companies (Fig. 12) are to be seen at the Salisbury and South Wiltshire Museum.

King James, on the many occasions when he came to Salisbury, stayed either at the Bishop's Palace, or at Sherborne Place, now called the King's House in his honour (Pl. 25). This old prebendal mansion of the Abbots of Sherborne, originally quite small, had been acquired in 1564 by Hugh Powell of Great Durnford, who incorporated several adjoining buildings in the house and greatly extended it on the north side. In 1588, a year after his death, in spite of legal difficulties, his widow Elihonor Powell was still living there. In 1596, at the age of fifty-three, she married Thomas Sadler as his second wife. Although eighteen years older than her new husband, she contrived to make him happy (as well as rich) and when she died at the age of nearly eighty he erected an effigy in the south aisle of the cathedral, where we see 'so good a wife and grave a matron' kneeling in black dress and white ruff near the spot where she 'served God daily nearly fifty years' (Pl. 19). Thomas Sadler held the office of Principal Registrar of the Diocese to six Bishops of Salisbury. He also added to the house on the south side, but these additions have largely disappeared. He and his wife entertained James I and his Queen more than once in their magnificent mansion, and the arms of the Prince of Wales in stained glass still adorn one of the windows. Sadler was knighted by King James in 1623.

In order to escape the plague raging in London, Charles I and his Court made a long stay in Salisbury in 1625. Stringent precautions were taken to prevent the dread sickness being brought in from outside. These succeeded for a time, but early in 1627 the plague arrived. In four days the city was deserted by all but the poorest people. The cathedral clergy shut themselves into the Close and platforms were built inside the Close wall so that they could climb up to be handed food. One man in authority remained, John Ivie, the Mayor. At a later date, when accused of high-handedness at this time, he wrote a detailed account of his experiences, to justify his actions, and this unique *Declaration* gives us a vivid picture of conditions in the city.

Two petty constables 'that had no friend to receive them in the country' stayed behind 'to help order the unruly bearers, and a multitude of rude people which was like both night and day to ruinate the whole City, but God being merciful unto us, did put into my heart to rule so great a multitude'. His wife and maid having been sent away to safety, Ivie's household consisted of his sergeant, one man, and an old serving maid who had been with him many years: 'we did all make a vow, and promise together, that whosoever it pleased God to visit of us, the other should be faithful unto him'.

With only £80 in his house to provide for three thousand people, Ivie's first act was to send to the justices outside for a contribution by law. He built storehouses in all three parishes and laid in wheat and barley, got a baker to work, and distributed bread and ale. He also built a pest-house, and took active steps to prevent looting. After having trouble with the watch and gaoling the ringleader with his own hands, Ivie gave orders that every man was to watch for his own house. But the main difficulty was to find bearers to carry corpses to the grave, because nobody would house the men. When the wife of one of the bearers was evicted by her landlord for fear of infection, Ivie threatened him with gaol, and had him carried half-way there before he gave in and agreed to reinstate the woman. The wretched bearers were persecuted by the mob and had both cold and scalding water thrown at them; small wonder that they went on strike and, armed with hedge stakes, asked for more than their four shillings a week a head. Ivie, never at a loss when it came to blows, 'look't about for stones in the street and put them into the skirt' of his gown until it was full and so a stoning match began, the Mayor being helped by the bystanders.

F

The men were driven into their cabin and then Ivie, armed this time with a musket, accused them of sheep-stealing. After one or two shots from his man the bearers, in fear of their lives, gave up the sheep, and Ivie promised them the shirts and Bibles for which they, oddly enough, were asking.

The most macabre scene of all occurred three days later when Ivie was summoned to the churchyard where he would see 'good sport' with the searching woman and the bearers. He goes on: 'I came to a place where I could see and hear them and . . . found the four Bearers, each of them having on their shoulders a Thurndel-pot of Ale. These five were dancing amongst the graves, singing "Hie for more shoulder-work" in a fearful manner.' When they saw the Mayor, they ran away and shortly afterwards one died; indeed nine bearers died that summer as the plague increased.

And the people drowned their fears in drink. With fifty inns and eighty ale-houses in the three parishes, Ivie suppressed nearly a hundred sellers of drink and 'by this course I did gain the ill-will of thousands of good and bad people'. The brewers, the bakers, all the hucksters, the cooks, and most of the innkeepers were 'mad', not to mention 'all the Drunkards, Whore-masters, and lewd fellows with their allies'. One ale-house where four journeymen weavers were lodged he was not able to suppress. These men bought a cowl of ale and drank it all, and the four men, together with the innkeeper, his wife, and his maid, were all dead in three days 'after their great drinking'. 'It pleased God', says Ivie, 'to give me power to suppress all, saving that one house; then the God of power did suppresse that house in his own judgement.'

But his troubles were not over. A 'base' woman, the widow Biby, 'desiring to do the Devil's work', set the pest-house on fire. When Ivie arrived, it was burnt down and he found the eighty-seven poor souls who had been in it 'sitting in the field upon the bare earth, in a miserable condition, many of them almost naked, and one of them quite naked'. They were clothed and sent back to their own houses and another pest-house was built.

It is recorded that 369 people died of the plague in two parishes, the figures for St Edmund's being unknown. John Ivie, by his firmness of character and ruthless methods no less than by his piety and compassion for the sufferers, cuts a heroic figure. The street where he is thought to have lived, in those days a part of New Street, is now named Ivy Street in his honour. In 1932 a plaque was unveiled to his memory in the Guild Hall which bears the following inscription:

In lasting memory of
John Ivie
Goldsmith
Mayor of the City of New Sarum
In the year 1627
When the City was sorely stricken
with plague

So that many citizens fled
For safety leaving him to bear
The burden of his office alone
Aided by two petty constables
Christopher Brathat and John Pinhorne.
'You have done your countrey good service
For which we are all beholding
To God and you.' [1]

Directly below this inscription is a beautiful old fire-place (Fig. 13) which has been in the Guild Hall ever since it was built in 1795. The fire-place, no longer connected with any chimney, was moved to its present position early in the nineteen-thirties. There is every reason to believe that it came from the old Council House, destroyed after the fire in 1780. The Elizabethan design and the arms of the City of Salisbury carved upon it form strong corroborative evidence of this tradition.

In contrast to the scenes of horror in Salisbury during the plague, the idyllic life being led by George Herbert at Bemerton only a few years later comes as a draught of clean water. It was in April 1630 that he was inducted into the living which he was to hold for less than three years, but in that short time left so ineffaceable a mark upon it that his saintly influence survives to this day. A distant kinsman of the Pembrokes, he had spent the early part of his life in scholastic circles at Cambridge, where he was Orator at the university. He moved much in Court society and had political ambitions at this time. But his health was always bad; as he himself put it, 'he had too thoughtful a wit; a wit like a penknife in too narrow a sheath, too sharp for his body'. And so in the course of time his mind turned more and more to spiritual things; he had been ordained deacon as early as 1626 but it was not until after much mental conflict that he finally decided to accept the living of Bemerton, which was offered to him by the King at the request of Philip, fourth Earl of Pembroke. Three months before, he had married Jane Danvers after a courtship lasting only three days, and it proved an ideally happy marriage. George Herbert rebuilt the parsonage at Bemerton and restored the little church adjoining it. Over the mantelshelf of the chimney in his hall he put these words, now engraved on the front of the house:

To my Successor.

If thou chance for to find
A new house to thy mind,
And built without cost;
Be good to the poor,
As God gives thee good store,
And then thy labour's not lost.

---

[1] According to Ivie, in his *Declaration* of 1661, the words quoted were addressed to him by the Salisbury Corporation on his work during the plague.

FIG. 13. Fire-place in the Guild Hall

Here he wrote most of his lovely religious poems and lived a life that will always be the ideal of the country parson: here he died of consumption in 1633 at the early age of thirty-nine.

There is one last picture of peace before we turn to the Civil War. His friend and biographer was Izaak Walton, and later in life the author of *The Compleat Angler* came often to Salisbury and stayed with his son and namesake, a canon of the cathedral who lived in the house now known as the Walton Canonry in the Close. It is pleasant to think of Piscator standing at the end of this beautiful garden, angling for trout and grayling in the Avon.

II

The troubles, long brewing, were now coming to a head. A reflection of the spirit of the times will be seen in the affair of Henry Sherfield and the window, to be recounted later, and was also manifested in different guise in a bitter quarrel in the Close over the appointment of a new music teacher for the choristers,[1] which aroused strong passions, when King Charles was called in to adjudicate between the Bishop and the Dean. In spite of the fact that Salisbury had entertained both King James and King Charles on so many occasions, the sympathies of its citizens were largely with Parliament.

Ship-money, levied by King Charles in 1635, had naturally been unpopular; John Dove the Mayor was indemnified by the corporation against any expense or loss he might incur in levying this tax, which was for 'providinge and furnishinge of a shippe of warr of the burden 700 tunnes for His Majestie's service to be provided by the Countye of Wiltes'. In religious matters, in spite of, or perhaps even because of the cathedral body (a somewhat unworthy one as revealed by Archbishop Laud's visitation of 1634), the city seems to have been strongly Protestant; Mr Caphman, a Protestant refugee from the Palatinate, was to be kept by the corporation during his stay in the city, each of 'the twenty-four' contributing two shillings a quarter and the 'forty-eight' twopence, for his support. As early as 1611 there had been friction between the city and the cathedral authorities. 'Mistris Maioresse and others the wyves of this whole companye' had been crowded out of the chapel which they attended in the cathedral and it was agreed that the beadle should have a new lock and key made, and should attend every Sunday to lock the ladies in so that they should no longer be troubled by 'others the in-habitants of the Close and Cittye'.

Ladies were even becoming vocal in church matters, and an enter-taining pamphlet was printed at a later date, in 1641, about 'A Dis-coverie of six Women Preachers', one of whom was Arabella Thomas, a Welshwoman living at Salisbury. On the title-page there is a quotation from 1 Corinthians xiv. 34, 35, in which St Paul puts women in their proper place, and which ends with the famous words: 'And if they will learne anything, let them ask their husbands at home; for it is a shame for women to speak in the Church'. However, Arabella not only spoke but preached a sermon saying 'that none but such painfull creatures as herself should goe to Heaven, for those Ministers which did not preach twice upon every Sabbath day . . . very shortly the black Raven by day, and the white Owle by night should scratch out their eyes'.

Church affairs loomed large at this period and many were the religious quarrels in Salisbury. The most famous of these was the one enacted at St Edmund's Church between the years 1629 and 1632. When Bishop Jewel, in 1567, ordered the replacement of 'idolatrous' coloured glass in churches by plain glass, a window representing the Creation on the south side of St Edmund's Church was for some reason allowed to remain. Early in 1629, at a vestry meeting at which the Vicar, two churchwardens, and five Justices of the Peace, as well as many parishioners, were present, Mr Henry Sherfield, Recorder of Salisbury, was given permission to take

[1] Told in the author's *Sarum Close*, Chapter XI (Cape, 1937).

down the offending window at his own expense and put in new plain glass. But two parishioners having expressed a wish to obtain the consent of the Bishop, Dr John Davenant, the latter promptly vetoed the idea when he heard what had happened in the vestry.

He had reckoned without the tender conscience of Mr Henry Sherfield. Sitting opposite to the window, he had been troubled by it for twenty years. So the following October the Recorder took the law into his own hands. One afternoon he got the sexton's wife to let him into the church. Shutting himself in, he climbed on the side of a pew and with a pikestaff proceeded to break the window in several places. Unfortunately the staff gave way and he fell four feet into the pew, hurting himself so severely that he lay there for a long time before being able to send for a horse to carry him home; there he remained for a month.

A storm ensued, not only in Salisbury but throughout the country, and culminated in proceedings taken by the Attorney-General against the Recorder (who was a bencher of Lincoln's Inn) in the Court of Star Chamber. The case came up on 6 and 8 February 1632, no fewer than twenty-two Privy Councillors being present, of whom eighteen gave separate judgments. In his own defence, Sherfield gave a description of the window (a replica of the latter in miniature is still preserved in St Edmund's vestry (Pl. 20)), and from the description we get an idea of the extraordinarily literal mentality of those times.

Mr Sherfield contended that the window was not a true representation of the Creation, 'for that it contained divers forms of little old men in blue and red coats, and naked in the heads, feet and hands, for the picture of God the Father; and that in one place he was set forth with a pair of compasses in his hands, laying them upon the sun and moon; and the painter had set Him forth creating the birds on the third day, and had placed the picture of beasts and men and women on the fifth day—the man was a naked man, and the woman naked in some part, as much from the knees upwards, rising out of the man'. The poor Recorder had found this all very confusing; the days of creation were out of their proper order; the woman was actually created out of a man's rib, and did not rise out of him; and worst of all, seven Gods were represented instead of one God. So in order to 'preserve a good conscience' and 'fearing that others might offend in idolatry' he had merely broken the little bits that were falsified, because they dishonoured God.

The judgment of Lord Cottington, Chancellor of the Exchequer, gives us a clue to the amount of feeling generated by the case. He likened the breaking of the window to the acts of the Puritans and Brownists; accused the Recorder of disobedience to, and contempt of, the Church, 'having thereby touched upon the royal power, and encroached upon the hierarchy of the bishops, who have their authority from the King'. He wanted Mr Sherfield to be removed from office, to make public acknow-ledgment of his fault in church, and pay a fine of £1,000 to the King.

Sir Thomas Richardson, Lord Chief Justice of the King's Bench, took a more lenient view, praising the good work the Recorder had done in the city, which Sir Thomas visited on circuit, and was so carried away by enthusiasm that he stated 'there is neither beggar nor drunkard there'. John Ivie could have told him a different tale.

The Earl of Pembroke, wisely perhaps, was among the four who declined to pass sentence. Finally a compromise was reached between the different judgments. Although eight Privy Councillors had agreed with the Chancellor in all his findings, nine agreed to the fine only; four others did not want any fine at all, four wanted a fine of 500 marks, and one wanted £500, 'which fine of £500 was taken for the king, because, according to the rules and orders of the Court of Star Chamber, where there was a difference of fines, the king was to have the middle fine'.

The church of St Edmund had the last word. In 1653 the tower fell, destroying the body of the church and with it the famous window. The present nave was the former chancel, which gives some idea of its original size; the tower, rebuilt under the Commonwealth, is one of the few examples of a Cromwellian church structure in England (Pl. 23).

With the beginning of the war in 1642 Salisbury looked to her defences. The Mayor and aldermen on 15 August took charge of the arms belonging to Lord Pembroke which had been brought into the town, and on the same day they ordered that all persons should be indemnified who worked on the fortifications and secured the ancient bounds. Further, the High Constables undertook to provide 'an able and sufficient watch and ward'. But these fortifications served little or no purpose: in 1642 the city was raided for valuables by Sir Edward Hungerford for the Parliamentarians and then occupied for a time by Sir William Waller. In 1643 came the turn of the Royalists under Lord Hertford. So far there had been no fighting in the city; that was to come later. In October 1644 Charles entered Salisbury at the head of 11,000 men and, being joined by Prince Rupert from Wilton, made a forced march on Andover, where he failed to overcome Waller's smaller force. It was not until 1645 that there was actual fighting in the streets, if we except a small skirmish at the end of 1644 between Ludlow's men and the Royalist force under Colonel Coke, who had hoped to fortify the Close. Ludlow remained in possession. One night the Royalists under Sir Marmaduke Langdale entered the city by Castle Street where, in Ludlow's own words, 'there was a great noise of horses'. Ludlow, after a brief reconnoitre, sallied forth from the Close with about thirty horsemen. Passing behind the Poultry Cross, he entered the Market Place by the narrow passage which we know today. The Royalists broke into two groups, and fled before him, one party making for Winchester Gate and the other passing up Endless Street. When they found it was a *cul-de-sac*, they turned on their pursuers. Eventually Ludlow was forced back to the Close and made his escape by Mrs Sadler's house (the King's House) to Harnham, leaving a small guard in the belfry. These men were smoked out by the Royalists, who backed a cart filled with charcoal against the door and set it on fire. The last episode we have to recount is the occupation of the city by Lord Goring in 1645, when for five weeks his Royalist troopers lived so riotously and practised such oppression on friend and foe alike that the sympathies of the town veered more and more to the Parliament.

Under the Commonwealth the Close fared badly. In 1647 the corpor-ation purchased the estates of the see which had been requisitioned by Parliament, the Bishop's Palace being used as an inn; in 1649 the Dean and Chapter lost their lands and the cathedral body was turned adrift, four canonry houses being bought for £880 to be used as parsonages for the Puritan ministers of the three city churches and the cathedral. The detailed survey of the houses in the Close taken in 1649 is most valuable to architects and historians.

Outside St Ann's Gate in St John Street is an ancient inn, the King's Arms, which played an important part in the escape of Charles II after the Battle of Worcester. From here plans were made by the Earl of Wilmot and Henry Peters in collaboration with Dr Humphrey Hench-man and Mr Coventry. Dr Henchman, the former precentor, still lived in the Close; at the Restoration he was to become Bishop of Salisbury, and be translated to London three years later. Mr Edward Coventry is thought to have lived in the house in the Close, now Number 15, which is immediately opposite to the King's Arms; the house is full of hiding-places (Pl. 22). In the garden is a summer-house in classical style. It is just conceivable that it was built as early as 1651 but is more likely to be of later date. In 1870 a secret chamber in the roof was discovered. A sliding panel gives access to it and in it were found a seventeenth-century horn tumbler, a mattress, and a handsomely embroidered blue velvet pillow which fell to pieces when touched. It is far more likely to have been used at the time of the Monmouth rebellion and it is certain that Charles himself was never there. He did not venture into Salisbury, which was a Puritan stronghold, but lay in hiding for several days at Heale House in the Avon valley until his friends in Salisbury had completed their plans for his escape to the Sussex coast, and thence to France. The owner of the house, the widow of Lawrence Hyde, recognized him and took the risk of hiding him. The day after his arrival, in fact, she sent him to Stonehenge until she had completed her preparations. The Hydes were staunch Royalists and Sir Robert Hyde, the Recorder of Salisbury, brother of Lawrence, was dismissed from office by the corporation owing to his sympathies. He was restored to office in 1660, and his effigy can be seen in the south transept of the cathedral. Their first cousin, the head of the family, was Edward Hyde, Lord Clarendon, the historian and statesman who was born at Dinton, possibly in the lovely little fifteenth-century house now owned by the National Trust, which is called Little Clarendon.

Life went on in Salisbury much as usual under the Commonwealth. The Mayor and Commonalty elected two members to Parliament 'in the usual place, being the Councell House' in July 1654, and eighteen months later took the precaution of petitioning the Lord Protector for the 'renewing and confirmation of the former Charters graunted to this Cittie'. Cromwell did not renew the charter until 1656; he did so, however, on account of the loyalty of the citizens and ordered the inhabitants of the Close to pay taxes to the corporation; at the same time he presented the city with a Sword of State and Cap of Maintenance. It was discovered in 1658 that brass farthings had been unlawfully 'minted and uttered'; they were called in, and a few months later a new official stamp for making them was ordered. Similarly a new seal had to be cut in 1658 to replace the common seal of the corporation stolen, with other things, from the Council House. The new one was to be as like as possible to the old, 'but with some addicion, as the date of the Lord'. The corporation might with advantage have turned their attention to more practical matters. The town was dirty. John Evelyn in 1654 noted that although the market-place and most of the streets were 'watered by a quick current and a pure stream running through the middle of them', they were 'negligently kept, when with small charge they might be purged and made one of ye sweetest towns, but now ye common buildings are despicable and ye streets dirty'.

It was an age not only of dirt, but of cruelty. Witch-hunts went on unabated, indeed they seem to have grown in ferocity at this time. In 1653 Anne Bodenham, aged eighty, was accused of having turned herself into a cat and then resumed her own shape; for this she was sentenced to death and executed at Fisherton Gaol. Another extraordinary story of 1659 illustrates not only the credulity of those days but also the powers of hypnotism and suggestion with which another 'witch' was endowed.

The tale was recounted by a justice of Malmesbury some twenty years after the event. On the refusal of the daughter of Hugh Bartholomew of Malmesbury to give her the yeast for which she had asked, the Widow Orchard went away, muttering to herself. Immediately the great cypress chest in the room above 'was lifted up and let fall so that it shook the whole house'. There was £200 in it and the 'gingling' of money was heard. Bartholomew rushed after the woman and accused her, but she said: 'You lie, you old Rogue; your chest is not broken, the nayles are only drawn and there is never a penny of your money gone'. This proved to be true. Three or four months later the widow was languishing in Salisbury Gaol for bewitching a gardener's daughter of Burbage. Orchard had asked the girl for food, but the latter, being faint with fatigue from pulling up and cleansing carrots, said she must wash, as her hands were sandy, and eat first herself. Orchard then three times trotted round the garden plot and squatted down, muttering unintelligible words. On her departure, the girl put her hands in water to wash, and at once 'her fingers were distorted in theyr joyntes, one this way, another that way, and with such extreme torment, that she cryed out as if one had been about to kill her . . . and say'd that wicked old woman had bewitched her'. The pursuit caught up with Orchard three days later at Edington and she was brought back to Burbage, where the girl was sleepless with pain and fever. Orchard said the girl must have washed her hands in unwholesome water; she had not bewitched her. Calling for some of the same water, she put a finger in it and made three circles 'contrary to the course of the Sun, and upon the mayd dipping her hands into it, the pain and distortion ceased but her fingers were left without strength'. The widow was taken to Salisbury and there convicted and executed for witchcraft.

Another witch, Margery Gingell, was hanged in distinguished company. 'For bewitching Ellianor Lyddiard to death' and 'for bewitching Anne Beedle so that she pined, and lamed' she suffered the extreme penalty on 3 May 1655 at the same time as the Salisbury victims of the Rising in the West.

Although the history books hardly mention it, this tragic story of heroism and failure is worth recounting in some detail. The prime movers in the Rising were Colonel John Penruddock of Compton Park, near Salisbury, and Colonel Hugh Grove of Chisenbury Priors. With King Charles himself pessimistic about the chances, and his special agents 'The Sealed Knot' considering a rising premature, these two gentlemen carried on with their plans, pinning their faith to promises of help from various quarters which did not materialize.

The original idea was to start on St Valentine's Day but the plan to attack Marlborough about 12–14 February had to be abandoned owing to the watchful eye of Colonel Boteler of that town. Nothing daunted, the Cavaliers made fresh plans; they met in Salisbury, according to the statements made to Secretary Thurlow by prisoners, either at the King's Arms or 'at the Lady Phillips' her house . . . and there they had directions what to do from the Lady Phillips, who came from London a little before, and had often been in France and other parts beyond the seas with the Queen'. This may have been Agneta Phelips of Montacute, whose husband Colonel Robin Phelips helped Charles to escape after Worcester. There was to have been a great horse race at Salisbury on 15 February where they were all to meet, but when this was stopped by Parliament they had to rely on meeting out fox-hunting to confer together.

At last the scheme was complete. Sir Joseph Wagstaffe, who was in command, arrived; men, horses, and arms were assembled; and on 11 March, a Sunday, they met in Clarendon Park, their strength being sixty, which swelled to a hundred with the addition of Thomas Mompesson's contingent. A detour to Blandford added eighty more, but the expected help from Hampshire did not arrive. Finally, fearing to wait longer, they marched on Salisbury, barely two hundred strong, with Sir Joseph Wagstaffe and Colonels Penruddock, Grove, and Jones at their head.

In the grey dawn of that March morning the little force entered the sleeping town. The Spring Assizes were in session, so there were extra people in the city, and not only people but horses. Posting some men in the market-place, the rebels put guards in all the inns; seized every available horse; broke open the gaol and recruited some of the prisoners, and, greatly daring, arrested Lord Chief Justice Rolle and Mr Baron Nicholas (the Judges of Assize) and the High Sheriff of Wiltshire, Mr John Dove, in their beds. Wagstaffe was for hanging the judges, but Colonel Penruddock pleading for their lives, they were shorn of their commissions and set free. The High Sheriff was kept as a hostage; refusing with tears to proclaim Charles II King, he received some rough treatment and was carried off in his night-shirt.

Meanwhile the citizens of Salisbury, on whose co-operation the Royalists had counted, stayed indoors in spite of Colonel Penruddock's speech announcing that the Duke of York was coming from France with ten thousand men and there was to be a rising in every county. There was no sign of the Marquis of Hertford with his promised contingent of horse and foot from Amesbury. Eventually the party, now some three hundred strong, made off through Downton to Blandford, where the unfortunate Mr Dove was allowed to dress; the Town Crier there refused to proclaim Charles II King, saying 'he could not say that word though they should call for faggots and burn him presently'. After a halt of two hours at Sherborne, they made for Yeovil, quartering there until 1 p.m. on Tuesday. There they let the Sheriff go. At last by way of Cullompton and Tiverton they reached South Molton, in Devon, at 7 p.m. on Wednesday. Utterly exhausted, they decided to stay the night. And then, three hours later, they were attacked by Captain Unton Crook from the garrison at Exeter with his troop of horse. The Royalists, depleted by the speed of their ride, had been reduced to a hundred men; Sir Joseph Wagstaffe fled in the darkness, and after a fight lasting several hours sixty or seventy gave themselves up, relying on Captain Unton Crook's promise that no harm should befall them. The prisoners were taken to Exeter Gaol.

No time was lost in bringing them to justice and trials were staged at Salisbury, Chard, and Exeter. Some of the less important prisoners were tried at Salisbury; among them were a vintner, an innholder, a cutler, a woollen-draper, a soap-boiler, a cloth-worker, a smith, two carpenters, a barber, a yeoman, a turner, a tailor, a spurrier, an ostler, and a 'milliner', which goes to show that the rising was by no means confined to the local gentry. Sir Joseph Wagstaffe was also tried, although absent, and in addition Thomas Mompesson, Saint Lowe, Richard Greene of Mere, and Mackes, a Salisbury apothecary, one of the ringleaders.

The city fathers had left no doubt as to which side they were on, sending a remonstrance to Cromwell to express 'their detestation of that traitorous insurrection, which first took fire within their walls through the insolence of a crew of desperate persons'. On 11 April there was a 'great appearance of honest jurymen' for the Sheriff to choose from; Colonels Penruddock and Jones had arrived from London, but two days later were sent on to Exeter. The interrupted Assizes were continued and the very judges who had received such short shrift, with the addition of four others, had the peculiar satisfaction of trying their own captors.

The little Council House must have been packed to bursting point. In addition to thirty prisoners, six judges, the lawyers, jurymen, witnesses, and the Sheriff's retinue, there were any number of soldiers—Colonel Boteler and his men, Unton Crook and his troopers, Major Ludlow and the Wiltshire Militia, and many more. Of the twenty-three on trial for treason, and seven more suspects who had been arrested as horse-stealers or highwaymen, seven, including Mackes, were sentenced to be hanged, drawn, and quartered, and eight to be hanged. Later there was a reprieve as regards drawing and quartering. On 3 May seven men were hanged, and Margery Gingell the witch perished with them.

It was on 19 April, at Exeter, that the ten most important trials took place, including those of Colonel John Penruddock and Colonel Hugh Grove. Very full accounts have survived and Penruddock's manuscript account of the proceedings is still in the possession of his descendants. In the course of an impassioned address to the jury he said: 'You are now Judges betweene mee and these Judges, let not the majesty of theyre lookes, or the glory of theyre habits, betray you to a sinne wch is of a deeper dye than their scarlett; I meane that sinne blood, wch calls to heaven for vengeance.' But it did not avail; the jury retired for only fifteen minutes and brought him in guilty.

Meanwhile Penruddock's wife Arundell was at Compton Park with her seven children. When he was first taken at Exeter, her husband had written to her asking for £100 for necessaries; he added 'my dear love, once more I beseech thee do not make myself and my poor children more unhappy by afflicting thyself for me. I have been used in the school of affliction and have learned in what estate soever I am to be therewithall content. Deliver my blessing to my poor children, seconded with your own. To close all, take my unfeigned love to yourself from Dear Heart Your loving husband J. Penruddock'. Now Arundell left her home and went to London to intercede for her husband's life. The devotion of these two is one of the greatest of love stories. In the portrait that still hangs at Compton Park (Pl. 27) we see them together, he a man of noble presence, his red-gold hair falling on his shoulders, she, although no beauty, with candour and steadfastness in her eyes and mouth. She petitioned the Protector by letter before the trial and in person after the condemnation. All she was able to accomplish was to have the sentence altered to one of beheading instead of hanging, drawing, and quartering. The death warrant was signed at Whitehall on 3 May 1655, and sent to Exeter.

That same night Arundell, out of the fullness of her heart, wrote the famous letter to her husband which has been immortalized by Sir Richard Steele in his essay, *The Lover*. This is what she wrote:

My dear heart,

    My sad parting was so far from making me to forget you, that I have scarce thought upon myself since, but wholly upon you. Those dear embraces which I yet feel, and shall never lose (being the faithful testimonies of an indulgent husband) have charmed my soul to such a reverence of your remembrances, that were it possible, I would with my own blood cement your dead limbs to life again, and with reverence think it no sin to rob heaven a little longer of a martyr. Oh my dear! You must now pardon my passion, tho' being the last (oh fatal word!) that ever you will receive from me; and know that until the last minute that I can imagine you shall live, I will sacrifice the prayers of a Christian, and the groans of an affected wife; and when you are not, which sure by sympathy I shall know, I shall wish my own dissolution with you, that so we may go hand in hand to heaven. It is too late to tell you what I have, or rather have not, done for you. How turned out of doors, because I came to beg for mercy! The Lord lay not your blood to their charge. I would fain discourse longer with you, but dare not, my passion begins to drown my reason, and will rob me of my devoir, which is all I have left to serve you.

Adieu therefore ten thousand times my dearest dear, and since I must never see you more, take this prayer 'May your faith be so strengthened, that constancy may continue, and then I hope heaven will receive you, where grief and love will in short time after, I hope, translate, my dear, your sad but constant wife, even to love your ashes when dead'.

                    A. Penruddock.

Your children beg your
blessing, and present
their duties to you.
     May the 3rd 1655 11 o'clock at night.

Colonel Penruddock was executed on 16 May. His family were not dispossessed of Compton Park and remained there for the best part of three hundred years.

After the Restoration the house was rebuilt, only a small portion of the original Tudor building remaining, and it was at this period that the lovely Grinling Gibbons library was made. At a later date the drawing-room with its perfect proportions was decorated in the most exquisite Adam style. But after the first world war the Penruddocks fell on evil days, and about ten years later the estate and house were sold to Mr George Cross, who spared neither pains nor money in restoring the dilapidated building to its former beauty.

Only five years after the abortive rising Charles II returned to England and was welcomed with acclamations by the country. Salisbury, like many another town, performed a *volte face* with considerable skill and agility. Cromwell's Sword of State was broken at the whipping-post and his Cap of Maintenance burnt. The council ordered 'that the Kinge's armes be newe sett up at the Cittye's charge in such manner as it was before the defaceing thereof on the North side of the Close Gate in the

Highstrete'. The dispossessed clergy returned and reoccupied the Close. Race-meetings were restarted and the council ordered a new race cup. It was our old friend John Ivie (a goldsmith by trade) who was to be 'intreated to procure the cupp to be had in due tyme before the race, and the Chamberlain is ordered to see payment made for the said cupp'.

Our last glimpse of the city at this time is through John Ivie's eyes. In his Declaration of 1661 he is in pessimistic mood, attributing the sad state of affairs to the 'late wicked war. Whereby', he says, 'we have such a mighty increase of lewd persons, and unruly poor, that our Government is at a stand: and I cannot hope to see God's Glory advanc't amongst us in this poor City whilst I live. For our poor do swarm about the City, Close and Countrey, and no restraint, whereby Bastardie is much increast, to the great grief of the inhabitants. . . .' If only, he mourns, his storehouses for the poor had not been abolished, things would have been different. There would not have been 'one Beggar in the City, nor none to want, nor no additional moneth made use of to grieve the inhabitants, nor none of any rank over-rated, but all should be, as in former time set to work, and their children bound apprentices, which hath been formerly done, and take all Beggars from the Inns, that are like sometimes to pull Travellers of any rank from their horses every morning, to the great scandal of our Government'.

There will always, in every community, be someone who laments the good old days. Better times were on the way, however, and the old city was to become before long a centre of Rank and Fashion where music, the arts, and literature flourished as never before.

IV

RESTORATION IN SALISBURY

1660–1790

WITH THE RESTORATION of King Charles II it must have seemed to the people of Salisbury as if the old days and old ways of the beginning of the century had returned; but, had they only known it, the greatest force for change since the coming of Christianity had appeared, namely, modern science, and Salisbury was to be a centre of the great scientific movement of the seventeenth century in England. Even the development of architecture, as seen in the formal grace and regularity of the late seventeenth- and eighteenth-century houses in the Close and city of Salisbury, reflects the changed habit of mind consequent upon this new way of thought.

After the strange aberration of the Commonwealth, the first bishop was Humphrey Henchman, formerly precentor of the cathedral, who had helped Charles II to escape after the Battle of Worcester. But in 1667, following the brief episcopates of John Earles and Alexander Hyde, a new bishop, Seth Ward, was appointed who was one of the central figures of the great scientific movement of the seventeenth century. He was born in the year 1617 in Hertfordshire and, having gone to Sidney Sussex College, Cambridge, in 1632, studied mathematics and became a mathematical lecturer there in 1643; and when the Master of his College was imprisoned in 1643 for his loyalty to King Charles I, Seth Ward attended him until his death. He was a staunch Anglican and collaborated with several others in compiling a book on *The Unlawfulness of the solemn League and Covenant*, which book was burned by the Puritans. In 1644 he was deprived of his fellowship. In 1648 John Greaves, Savilian Professor of Astronomy at Oxford, was ejected by the Puritans, and Seth Ward, who was now a well-known mathematician and astronomer, was appointed to succeed him in this professorship. Ward had been ordained to the Anglican ministry, and gained fame both as a lecturer on astronomy and as a preacher. He published an important theory of the elliptical nature of the planetary orbits in 1653, and a famous book called *De Astronomia Geometrica* in 1656. He had in 1650 become Fellow of Wadham

College, Oxford, which just at that time was a centre of pioneer scientific thought, under John Wilkins, later Bishop of Chester. Among the circle of inquirers and experimenters who gathered at this college were Robert Boyle, Thomas Willis, John Wallace, Ralph Bathurst, and Lawrence Rooke. In 1649 this group of scholars formed the Philosophical Society of Oxford, one of the two parent societies from which arose the world' famous Royal Society. Thus, Seth Ward was one of the original members of the Royal Society. Among his students at Oxford was Sir Christopher Wren, and in 1671 it was Bishop Seth Ward who proposed Sir Isaac Newton, 'Professor of the Mathematics' at Cambridge, for fellowship of the Royal Society.

During his time at Oxford Seth Ward became involved in mathe' matical and philosophical controversies with the famous Wiltshire philosopher, Thomas Hobbes of Malmesbury. In 1654 Ward took his D.D. degree at Oxford and in 1657 was elected Principal of Jesus College; but Cromwell refused to agree to his appointment. In 1660 Ward resigned his professorship and became Vicar of St Lawrence Jewry. In 1656 he had been appointed by the exiled Bishop of Exeter to the position of Precentor of Exeter Cathedral, if the Bishop should be restored. In 1660 this was duly confirmed; in 1661 Ward became Dean of Exeter, and in 1662 was made Bishop of the same diocese. He cleansed Exeter Cathedral, restored and beautified it, and installed a new pair of organs.

Like the other experimental scientists of his time, Seth Ward was a personal friend of Charles II, and all the more so in view of his loyalty to Charles I. It was, therefore, not surprising that five years later he was appointed Bishop of Salisbury. He came from Exeter with a reputation not only for sound learning but also for hard and conscientious work among the clergy of his diocese, and a vigorous enthusiasm for the care and restoration of sacred buildings; and these same virtues he displayed in Salisbury. His first act after coming to the see was to beautify his cathedral and palace. In 1669 he invited his friend and pupil, Sir Christo' pher Wren, to make a survey of the cathedral; and the manuscript notebook containing this survey is preserved to this day in the cathedral library. Wren made several suggestions for the improvement and repair of the cathedral, though his opinion of the general design of the building was high and he records his praise of the first architect:

whose judgment I must justly commend for many things, beyond what I find in divers Gothick Fabricks of later date which, tho' more elaborated with nice and small workes, yet want ye natural beauty which arises from Proportion of ye first dimensions. For here, the breadth to the heighth of ye Navis, and both to ye Shape of the Iles beare a good proportion. The Pillars and ye Spaces between them are well suited to ye highth of the Arches, the Mouldings are decently mixed with large planes without an affectation of filling every corner with ornaments, which (unlesse they are admirably good) glut ye eye, as much as in Musick, too much Division cloyes ye eare, the Windowes are not made too great, nor yet ye light obstructed with many mullions and transomes of Tracery-worke which was ye ill fashion of ye next (following) age. Our Artist knew better that nothing could adde beauty to light, he trusted in a stately and rich Plainenesse.

The splendid Hall adjoining Braybrooke House, Number 57 The Close, which was afterwards the Choristers' School, may possibly have been built by Wren (Pl. 31).

In 1672 Bishop Seth Ward gave a large sum towards the scheme for making the River Avon navigable from Salisbury to the sea which, after many controversies, was at last successful, so that by 1684 two vessels laden with twenty-five tons could be brought up to Crane Bridge. Seth Ward was a most conscientious bishop in the care of his diocese, visiting his clergy assiduously and doing much to try to improve the incomes of the poorer benefices. As he journeyed about he made notes of his impressions of the clergy and of their diligence, and entered these in a large notebook. This notebook, which also contains a vast amount of miscellaneous information, including a number of remarkable formulae for patent medicines, in which Ward showed a scientific interest, is still preserved among the bishop's archives, and a fine manuscript copy of it exists in the cathedral library.

Seth Ward had many improvements made in the cathedral, 'first at his proper charges', as Dr Pope says, 'paving the Cloisters, then at his exhortation and expense the paving of the church was mended where it was faulty, and the whole choir laid with white and black squares of marble, the Bishop's throne and all the prebends' stalls being made new and magnificent. His next care was to repair, I might almost say rebuild, his Palace, which was much ruined, the hall being pulled down and the greatest part converted to an Inn, what remained of it being divided into small tenements. Bishop Ward's expenses in altering, repairing, and rebuilding the Palace amounted to above £2,000'.

During his sojourn at the palace he had for a time as his domestic chaplain a great fellow mathematician, Isaac Barrow, later Master of Trinity College, Cambridge, who was one of the most famous of all the scientists of that great period, and was for several years a canon and prebendary of Salisbury Cathedral. Many other scientists visited Seth Ward at Salisbury, among them Robert Boyle from his house at Stal-bridge, who, when he died, is reputed to have been charmingly described on his tomb as 'the Father of Chemistry and the Uncle of the Earl of Cork'.

Another Fellow of the Royal Society who visited Salisbury and 'looked in and saw the Bishop, my friend Dr Ward' was Samuel Pepys, who in 1668 stayed at the Old George Inn, where he 'lay in a silke bed and had very good diet. The next morning Hewer and I up and down the town and find it a very brave place. The river goes through every street; and a most capacious market-place. . . . The Minster most

G

admirable, as big, I think, and handsomer than Westminster . . . a very good organ'. He made two attempts to see the choir, which failed, owing to the devotion of the choirmen, who were at prayers, so he contented himself with an inspection of the 'very fine tombs, some very ancient of the Montagus'; and on returning to the George Inn found the reckoning so exorbitant that he and his family moved immediately to a small place just outside Salisbury where 'the beds were good but lousy, which made us merry'.

Seth Ward, having been loyal to the Church of England when it was almost overwhelmed by Puritan schismatics, was not unnaturally appre- hensive of the disloyal and disruptive influence of dissenters; but though he opposed the nonconformists in general, he showed great kindness and forbearance to individual ministers, and had great regard to true piety. He was accused of persecuting nonconformists, but no clear evidence exists of this. Towards the end of his life he was unfortunately involved in a bitter dispute with the Dean of the cathedral, Dean Pierce, and the strain of this 'black malice of the Dean of Sarum' ultimately impaired his mind. When he died in 1688/9 he left to the cathedral library a splendid collec- tion of sixteenth- and seventeenth-century scientific, mathematical, and astronomical books which he had acquired during his life, and this unique collection is still preserved there. John Aubrey, the diverting author of the *Brief Lives*, and himself a Wiltshireman, describes Seth Ward thus: 'He is a batchelour, and of a most magnificent and munificent mind. . . . He had an admirable habit of body (athletique, which was a fault), a handsome man, pleasant and sanguine; he did not desire to have his wisdome be judged by the gravity of his beard, but his prudence and ratiotination.'

His death in 1688/9 deprived Salisbury of one of the most distinguished, intelligent, and conscientious bishops it ever knew, and he died greatly beloved both by the townsfolk and by his clergy. He was courtly in manner, much given to hospitality, and generous in private life. In addition to his work in beautifying and preserving the cathedral and its spire, he also in 1682 bestowed upon the Close a very lovely building just inside the High Street gate, known as the Matrons' College (Pl. 24)—a charity created by him to provide a home for twelve widows of clergy from his own two dioceses of Salisbury and Exeter, and still used for this purpose today. It is said that he was moved to found this college because in early youth he had proposed marriage to a lady who had refused him and who, after marrying a clergyman in Exeter diocese, was left a widow in poverty. To provide a home for her, Seth Ward built the Matrons' College.

Later on, in 1712, special seats were provided in the cathedral for the inmates of this college by Sir Stephen Fox. This worthy gentleman was born at Farley, near Salisbury, and, as John Evelyn says, 'came first a poor boy from the quire'; but later he rose to be Member of Parliament for

Salisbury on three separate occasions, in 1661, 1685, and for the last time in 1714, when he was 86 years of age. He was also Paymaster to the Army and one of the Lords Commissioners of the Treasury. He married for the second time at the age of 76 and one of the four children of this marriage was the father of the Whig statesman, Charles James Fox. He was a most generous man, who gave £13,000 towards the construction of Chelsea Hospital, and he built a set of singularly lovely almshouses and a wardenry at the village of Farley, and also gave the church there, a particularly fine example of seventeenth-century ecclesiastical architecture, said to have been built to some extent under the supervision of Sir Christopher Wren.

It may be mentioned here that several of the other ancient almshouses for which Salisbury may justly be called remarkable were erected about this date: in 1682 Margaret Blechynden's almshouse was built in Winchester Street for six widows who were 'industrious, of good conversation and above the age of 50', and though much altered, this building can still be seen on the same site; Sutton's almshouses were erected in 1699 in St Ann Street for 'three poor weavers and their widows after them'; Taylor's almshouse, for '6 poor single men of the city', was built in Bedwin Street in 1695; and Frowd's was erected in 1720 at the corner of Church Street and Rollestone Street. In addition there are five almshouses still extant in Salisbury, all of which are of an earlier date than these. Some of them, such as the Trinity almshouses (Pl. 10), rebuilt in 1707, were restored during this period.

Turning again to Seth Ward and his circle, it is safe to assume that among those with whom the Bishop must have enjoyed intelligent conversation on natural science was Isaac Walton (the son of the author of *The Compleat Angler*), who was then a canon of the cathedral. He lived in a singularly beautiful house on the west side of the Close, Number 69, which is one of the loveliest of the seventeenth-century houses which add such glory to the Close. Another scientific man of that age, whose fame spread beyond the confines of England, was Dr Turberville, the famous eye specialist, who also lived in the Close at Salisbury. According to Dr Pope, the friend and biographer of Bishop Seth Ward, Dr Turberville 'was no boaster, nor would he promise to cure any distemper. . . . He generally prescribed to all, shaving their heads, and taking tobacco, which he had often known do much good, and never any harm to the eyes'. His arrival in Salisbury from London was a source of great benefit, not only to those afflicted with optical diseases, but also to the innkeepers who catered for them, 'insomuch that one could scarce peep out of doors, but he had a prospect of some led by boys or women, others with bandages over one or both eyes, and yet a greater number wearing green silk upon their faces, which, if a stranger should see without knowing the reason for that phenomenon, I should not wonder if he believed the air of Sarum to be as pernicious to the eyes as that of

Orleans is to the nerves, where almost one-third of the inhabitants are lame. The rendezvous of these hoodwinked people was at the Doctor's. . . .'

Among other Fellows of the Royal Society in the days of Seth Ward was Joseph Glanvil, whose book *Sadducismus Triumphatus* includes a remarkable description of the peculiar phenomena which occurred at the house of Mr John Mompesson at Tidworth, in connection with the person known as the 'Daemon Drummer of Tedworth'. These phenomena are discussed in many modern books on poltergeists. The Mompesson family, however, left far more tangible relics of themselves in the Close: in the cathedral itself there is to be seen the magnificent tomb of Sir Richard Mompesson and his wife, while on the north side of the Close, overlooking the Choristers' Green, is the superb seventeenth-century house built by Mr Thomas Mompesson (Pl. 33), who moved here from Bathampton House, near Wylye. It was built upon a piece of ground rented to Mr Mompesson by the Dean and Chapter in 1681, and appears to have replaced an earlier house on this site. An interesting point about it is that it has the original lead rainwater heads and downspouts, bearing the date 1701. This lead work fashioned by artist craftsmen of the early eighteenth century is an element of beauty as well as of utility. The wrought-iron gates and delicate lamp carriers, which are fine examples of the smith's art, have elaborate scroll work, and the interior has beautifully carved balusters to the staircase and fine plaster work in the ceilings. The house was apparently completed in the year 1701. From 1946 to 1951 it was the residence of the Bishop of the Diocese; and it is now the property of the National Trust.

Another person of note in a different sphere at the same period was Michael Wise, who was organist of Salisbury Cathedral from 1668 to 1687. He was one of the first of the 'Children of the Chapel Royal', and in 1676 was made a 'Gentleman' of the same Chapel. He was a composer of considerable note, and is described by Dr E. H. Fellowes as 'one of the four leading English composers of the Restoration period'. He did not compose very many works, but 'his compositions are much superior to those of most of his contemporaries'. He was probably born at Salisbury about 1648, and four of his anthems are still performed regularly in the cathedral. He was a man of very difficult and irascible disposition, a fact which led to his death, since, after quarrelling one night with his wife, he rushed out into the street and 'gave stubborne and refractory language' to the night-watch; and by them he was 'knock'd on the head and kill'd downright on St Bartholomew's Day'.

In 1665, when the Great Plague broke out in London, King Charles II decided to move from that city to Salisbury and established his court here in August of the same year, as mentioned by Samuel Pepys in his diary. Although he stayed here for only a short time and the next month moved to Oxford, the sum of £100 was borrowed for providing 'presents of plate and money to the King and Queens' Majesties at their coming to this City'. Unfortunately, the plague followed in the royal train to Salisbury, though it does not appear to have been severe in that year. In 1666 a worse outbreak took place, and it is recorded that the election of the mayor and other officers was not held in the city 'by reason of the great infection of the plague about this time', but was performed at an assembly of the common council in the Close (Pl. 26).

In 1669 Salisbury was honoured by another distinguished visitor, Cosimo de Medici, hereditary Prince of Tuscany. He stayed at Wilton and was entertained by the Earl of Pembroke, but was clearly interested in the attractions which Salisbury had to offer, in particular the cathedral (Pl. 28), which he described as 'Gothic in all its parts, yet magnificent and sumptuous and considered with reason as one of the most beautiful temples in England'. His chronicler also remarks that 'the rivers Avon and Nadder, being diverted from their natural course, run in several channels through the City, traversing the streets, and forming several islands, which are made into gardens. The Church and the Square, in which is the Town-house, bear away the palm, amongst the most remarkable things which it contains'. The 'Town-house' was the old Council House, which at this time stood in the Market Square.

The reference here to the rivers flowing through Salisbury is amplified by the description of the city given by Celia Fiennes, who was born at Newton Tony, a village a few miles to the north, in 1662, and who in 1685 came to the city on one of her famous journeys. 'Pretty large town streetes broad but through the midst of them runs a little rivulet of water which makes the streetes not so clean or so easye to passe in, they have stepp's to cross it and many open places for horses and carriages to cross itt—it takes off much from the beauty of the streets. . . . There is a large Market House with the Town Hall over it and a prison just by, there is also a large Cross in another place and house over it for a constant Market for fruite, fowle, butter and cheese and a fish Market. The town is well served with all provissions, there is good buildings in that part they call the Close both new built and the old good houses belonging to the doctors of the Church.'

Between 1675 and 1677 new charters were granted to a number of merchant companies in the city, including the Clothworkers and Bakers, the Cooks and the Tallowchandlers, the Glovers, the Collarmakers, the Sievemakers, the Joiners, and the Hammermen. The above list of trade guilds in Salisbury at this period gives a good idea of the commercial activities of the city at the time; but the clothing industries began to decline in prosperity soon after the turn of the century.

In 1684 James, Duke of York, afterwards James II, came over from Winchester with his Duchess and the Princess Anne, to visit Salisbury, when 'a treat of sweetmeats and wine' was provided at the Council House. In 1685 the city was prompt in expressing its loyalty and attachment to this new king, who in March of that year granted it a new charter. It is not surprising that the people of Salisbury gave no support to the rebellion of the Duke of Monmouth. When Judge Jeffreys visited the city in 1685 we are told that the 'proceedings were so light, in comparison of the memorable punishments then immediately in prospect, that the judges might almost have demanded the pair of white gloves'. With a view to increasing the loyalty of the West of England, King James II decided to make a journey thither in person, and on his way visited Salisbury in 1686. When William, Prince of Orange, landed in Devon-shire in October two years later, three regiments of horse set out to join him, but their old loyalty to James II proved too strong and they returned to Salisbury, where they laid down their arms to the King. The greater part of the army, however, still left at Salisbury to resist the advance of William from Exeter, soon joined the rebellion, and among others who deserted James was Lord Churchill, afterwards Duke of Marlborough. At this critical time Salisbury was the headquarters of King James, who stayed in the episcopal palace; while there his activities and decisions were impeded by a severe nose-bleeding lasting for almost two days; but on 22 November 1688 he left the city with all speed for Windsor. On 4 December William of Orange, with his Dutch troops, entered the city and was met by the Mayor and aldermen and the army with great cere-mony. He stayed for only one night in Salisbury at the Bishop's Palace, and then proceeded to Oxford.

In 1689 the See of Salisbury was vacant owing to the death of Bishop Seth Ward, and William appointed to the bishopric a staunch supporter of the Protestant cause, Gilbert Burnet. Bishop Burnet was a well-known and eminent historian. Of Scottish birth, he had originally been a Presbyterian, and, though he had early joined the Church of England, he always retained somewhat of a Presbyterian outlook. During his career he worked constantly for union between the Anglicans and the non-conformists and was a prominent member of the protestant or reforming party in the Church of England and a Whig in politics. In spite of his rather loose adherence to Anglican principles and the fact that he was very intolerant of the high church party, Bishop Burnet was a good, intelligent, and conscientious Bishop of Salisbury, and his support of those natural sciences, so notably practised by Bishop Seth Ward, can be deduced from the magnificent funeral sermon which he preached on the death of Robert Boyle. An interesting figure in the diocese during his episcopate was John Norris, a good poet and a very eminent English philosopher, who first introduced the philosophy of Malebranche into this country. He shared the ecclesiastical views of Bishop Seth Ward and, therefore, did not meet with the approval of Bishop Burnet. He had, as he once remarked, 'a fine prospect of Salisbury Cathedral from his garden at Bemerton Rectory, and that was the only prospect he possessed in respect of that Cathedral'.

In the early years of the eighteenth century a considerable amount of building took place in the Close and elsewhere in Salisbury. The present Council House (Pl. 32) on Bourne Hill, on the site of the former College of St Edmund, dates from the late seventeenth century, but Barnard's Cross and the New Hall in New Street are eighteenth-century buildings. Many of the houses of the Close were altered and refronted, so that some of the oldest, for example the Hungerford Chantry (Number 54), were given a façade of Queen Anne style, although they are in fact of much earlier date. Several of the most beautiful houses in the Close, such as those in the northwest corner around the Choristers' Green, Mompesson House, Numbers 54, 55, and 56 (Hemingsby), acquired their present appearance at this time. Other fine examples of late seventeenth-century and eighteenth-century architecture in the Close are the Theological College (Number 19); Arundells (Number 60), built in 1749; Braybrooke House (Number 47) built in 1718; Audley House (Number 64); the Walton Canonry (Number 69) rebuilt in 1714; and Numbers 36 and 38, the latter of which has a Queen Anne front and an Elizabethan interior. Another fine house of this period is Myles's Place (Number 68), which was built in 1718 by William Swanton. Shortly afterwards it was occupied by Dr Heale, who was the first physician at the Salisbury Infirmary. The original portion of the Infirmary was constructed in 1767–1771, by the famous architect Wood of Bath, and is a fine example of public architecture and a comparatively early city hospital. Dr Heale was succeeded by Dr John Jacob, who had previously been his assistant, and Number 68 has been inhabited by the Jacob family from that time until the present day.

One of the literary associations of Salisbury arises from the fact that at Number 14 The Close, the house on the south side of St Ann's Gate, lived Henry Fielding, whose connection with Salisbury was due to his maternal grandmother, Lady Gould, with whom he used to stay; and he married Miss Charlotte Cradock, a Salisbury lady. A further though less directly literary association of Salisbury concerns a man named Jarvis Matchem, who in 1786 confessed to murdering a drummer boy on Salisbury Plain seven years before, and stated that he had been driven to confess by spectres which he had seen when crossing the Plain to Salisbury. This story was retold by R. H. Barham in the *Ingoldsby Legends* under the title of 'The Drummer of Salisbury Plain'.

At Number 15 The Close (Pls. 22 and 29), lived James Harris (the father of Lord Malmesbury), who, although he was a very gifted and intelligent man, aroused Dr Johnson's ire and was described by him as 'a prig and a bad prig'. In 1733 he took up residence in the Close in the house of his father, also named James Harris, and for the next fifty years was the leader of all the social life there, on one occasion in 1761 entertaining the Duke of York for the night at his house. But although he was a popular and a social figure, and kept up 'constant and cheerful intercourse with his neighbours', he placed his 'chief happiness in the care of his family, and after that in literature'. Under his auspices an annual musical festival flourished in Salisbury and subscription concerts were organized. It is said that George Frederick Handel, who was his father's friend, gave his first concert in England in the room over the St Ann's gateway (Pl. 38) adjoining the Harris house in 1710.

These Salisbury Subscription Concerts later became the cause of a celebrated local feud. In 1780 the organist of the cathedral, another Mr Harris, died, and rival claimants for this position arose in the persons of Joseph Corfe and Robert Parry, the former supported by the Dean, the latter by the Canons. Parry was appointed by a majority of votes of the Chapter, and Corfe was extremely disgruntled. Three weeks later, however, he was somewhat mollified by being made 'conductor of the band' which gave the subscription concerts; to meet this threat to his popularity, Mr Parry organized rival concerts. After a time, owing to the pugnacious attitude of some of Mr Corfe's friends, these were held not in the Assembly Room, but in 'Mr Gibbin's room in the New Canal'. In 1782 Mr Corfe was distinguished by being made a Gentleman of the Chapel Royal: not to be outdone, Mr Parry obtained the post of principal bass singer at the 'Concert of Ancient Music, Oratorios, etc.' in London. The feud ended only in 1792 when Parry died and Corfe was elected organist in his place.

A similar rivalry developed in the matter of elegant academies for young ladies. Of these there were two in the Close, one at the Hungerford Chantry, run by Mrs Stephens and Mrs Ivie, and the other at the King's House, run by Mrs Smith; and at these two establishments two dancing masters exercised their talents and at the same time strove to gain the favour and patronage of the young gentlemen from the Cathedral School, whom they also wished to instruct in the art of dancing. The rivalry between these two and between the ladies assumed entertainingly large proportions, as issues of the *Salisbury Journal* for the year 1769 reveal, both sides inserting advertisements to prove their superiority.

In addition to these fashionable academies for young ladies in the Close, Dr Godolphin in 1720 made a bequest for the care and education of eight young gentlewomen 'so born', whose parents were members of the Church of England and whose fortunes did not exceed £300. From this arose the Godolphin School for Girls, which has now become a famous public school. Owing to legal delays in connection with the bequest, the school was not actually in being until 1784. But educational activities were by no means confined to schools, and in the last quarter of the century anyone wishing to improve his education had many and various methods of doing so. He could belong to the Literary Society, formed in 1774, which met at the Maidenhead Inn; he could attend a course of scientific lectures by Mr Warltire; he could pay a visit to the Assembly Rooms where the celebrated Miss Lindley had appeared to entertain; he could be instructed in astronomy by Mr Flower; he could view the 'Ethiopian Savage' who was on show at the Vine Inn.

A further possible source of instruction and enlightenment may have been found in the first local newspaper, which was published in 1715 and called the *Salisbury Postman*. An incident no doubt described in this paper, if it was still extant, was the visit to Salisbury in 1722 of King George I, who was received by the Mayor and Corporation at the Winchester Gate, now no longer standing. In 1729 the *Salisbury Journal* was first published by Mr William Collins, and nineteen years later its office was moved to the present site in the New Canal. It now claims to be the oldest English newspaper still in private ownership. It has been connected with the Bennett family since 1848 and in its office a copy of the original issue of the paper is still preserved. One of the occasions no doubt recorded in this paper was the visit to Salisbury of John Wesley, who preached in Church Street in 1776. It is interesting to note that Oliver Goldsmith's *Vicar of Wakefield* was published by Benjamin Collins of Salisbury in 1766.

During the eighteenth century a further artistic development took place in connection with the theatre in Salisbury. In 1706 stage players had been prohibited from entering the city, but in 1747 a group of schoolboys acted *The Orphans*, and various strolling players visited the city. In 1751–2 one of Hallam's companies played a series of Shakespeare's plays, includ' ing *Romeo and Juliet*, *King Lear*, *Othello*, and *Hamlet*; and in the following year a company from Bath appeared, performing, among other things, Sheridan's *The Recruiting Officer*. All these performances took place in a converted room in the Vine Inn, near to the Cheese Cross. By 1765 there was another theatre at the Sun Inn in Fisherton Street, where the Maundrel Hall now stands, and in 1777 the New Street Playhouse was opened, which stood approximately on the site of the present Art School. From that time onwards plays were performed regularly here and a permanent company was founded which visited Winchester, Chichester, and Southampton. The programmes consisted always of a play followed by a farce, and after the play it was possible to get in for half price—a fact which most likely accounted for such notices as this one of 1778: 'It is humbly requested of gentlemen that they would for the future indulge their friends at the old Vine Pothouse, and not at the New Theatre, Salisbury.' The Vine Inn theatre received the honour of a visit from Lord Pembroke and Mr David Garrick in 1770. The play performed was *The Provok'd Husband*, and the distinguished visitors 'expressed the highest satisfaction at the comedians' endeavours to please'.

The eighteenth century was not only a period of considerable activity in the erection of new buildings (Pl. 30): it was also a time when much restoration work was carried out. In 1711 the ancient Poultry Cross was 'repaired and beautified' (Pl. 35). In 1741 the cathedral spire was struck by lightning and set on fire, and, possibly as a result of this, though mainly as a result of years of neglect in the early eighteenth century, it became necessary to carry out extensive repairs to the cathedral. After the death of Bishop Burnet a series of bishops had been appointed to Salisbury who either spent most of their time in London or were very elderly at the time of their appointment. From 1723 to 1734 the Bishop of the Diocese was Benjamin Hoadly—a singularly unpleasant example of a pompous, worldly, latitudinarian divine of the eighteenth century. He owed his appointment entirely to political influence and an accommodating nature, and possessed scarcely any of the characteristics proper to a bishop. His personality is immortalized for all time in an extremely penetrating and amusing portrait by William Hogarth. He was succeeded by a bishop of very different calibre, Thomas Sherlock, a conscientious man of very sound views, who was, however, handicapped by ill health. From 1748 to 1757 the see was occupied by John Gilbert, later Archbishop of York, and in 1761 Robert Drummond was appointed, who did much to repair and improve the Bishop's Palace, but who was unfortunately moved to York in the same year. His successor, John Thomas, the second Bishop of Salisbury of this name, was married four times, and attributed the shortness of his wives' lives to the fact that he always let them have their own way. An unfailing optimist, he had as the motto on his fourth wedding ring the words: 'If I survive, I'll make them five'. He did not! John Hume, who was appointed to succeed him in 1766, began alterations in the cathedral by removing the choir stalls which had been erected in the time of Wren, and he was followed in 1782 by another man who possessed this same desire to repair and restore, Shute Barrington. Bishop Barrington spent vast sums enlarging the palace, and took a big piece of the cathedral churchyard into its grounds, so depriving the public of one of the loveliest views of the cathedral—that from the south, with the Chapter House in the foreground. Having completed his work on the palace, he decided to effect repairs upon the cathedral itself, and for this purpose he employed the famous eighteenthcentury architect James Wyatt.

This was not the first attempt at restoration in the eighteenth century. Previous repairs had been carried out from 1777 to 1779, when the cathedral was closed, though it was opened to greet George III and his Queen in 1778, when they stayed at the Bishop's Palace and received there the Mayor and Corporation, afterwards attending a short concert in the cathedral. During these alterations the Hungerford Iron Chantry, erected in 1429, in the northeast corner of the nave, was removed to its present position on the south side of the sanctuary, by the Earl of Radnor, who converted it into his family pew. The choir itself was encased by a wooden screen on the north and south.

In 1788 Wyatt commenced his work of restoration, which was completed three years later. By way of encouragement, King George III presented an organ to the cathedral (which was subsequently removed to make way for the present Victorian instrument and placed in St Thomas's Church). The previous organ had been installed in 1710. The Act Books of the Chapter for the years 1789–91 give full details of the work proposed, and make it clear that the main instigator of the whole scheme was not so much Wyatt himself as Bishop Shute Barrington. In fact, there is evidence that Wyatt did not approve of the destructions he was compelled to carry out at Salisbury. These included the removal of the ancient bell tower (Pl. 34), which formerly stood on the site of the path leading from the Choristers' Green to the northwest porch, and very close to the little house named Ladywell. This belfry had long fallen into a very bad state of repair, having suffered damage during Ludlow's military operations in 1644–5 and deteriorated ever since. It is doubtful whether it had been much used since the time of the Commonwealth. Since at least the early part of the seventeenth century the lower part of it had been an ale-house, and a favourite pastime on Whit Monday was to go up to the belfry and 'jamble' the bells. It is known that in 1746 two of the bells were already cracked as a result of this, and in 1758 the Chapter had ordered the two top storeys to be taken down. By 1777 six of the bells had been sold to raise money; and the only remaining bell now hangs in the cathedral tower and is tolled for services. It is clear that the repair of the belfry would have involved its rebuilding and either the recasting or replacing of the bells. Wyatt considered, perhaps rightly, that the large and high bell tower obscured the grand view of the cathedral to be obtained from the Choristers' Green, and thought it best to pull the belfry down and remove it. Subsequently Bishop Shute Barrington had the whole of the churchyard raised and levelled, the graves being grassed over. This provoked great indignation from the townsfolk, but has left for posterity the fine expanse of lawn now surrounding the cathedral. It was certainly necessary to cleanse the churchyard, for in 1782 John Byng had written of Salisbury: 'The Churchyard is like a cow-common, as dirty and as neglected, and through the centre stagnates a boggy ditch.'

Two other demolitions which Wyatt carried out had, he argued, a similar practical justification—the destruction of the beautiful fifteenth-century Hungerford and Beauchamp Chantry Chapels, which stood one at each end of the choir aisles. The Chapter Minutes of November 1789 record the agreement of the Chapter to the plan of taking down the Hungerford and Beauchamp chantry chapels and rebuilding and making good the walls and buttresses to the church. It was this part of Wyatt's plan which naturally aroused such furious opposition, Horace Walpole, among others, being particularly vehement in his criticism. Here again we should remember that these chapels had not been used since the Civil War. They were reported to be unsafe and the cost of restoration would have been great. Thirty years earlier the cathedral surveyor had reported that the building of tombs into the walls of the Lady Chapel from these chantry chapels had weakened the whole Lady

Chapel, and it is reasonable to suppose that one of Wyatt's objects was to preserve and strengthen the Lady Chapel, which many competent judges today consider to be the finest piece of architecture in the interior of the cathedral. The method by which the removal of these chantry chapels was carried out is greatly to be deplored. On the other hand, it is to be remem-bered that at the present day we can claim that the whole interior of Salisbury Cathedral was built at one and the same time to the design of one man, Elias de Dereham, and that it has an unimpaired unity. This claim could not have been made while the Hungerford and Beauchamp chantry chapels and the porches still stood. In removing these excrescences, Wyatt was aiming at restoring the original simplicity and unity which had undoubtedly been the intention of Elias de Dereham himself.

Similarly, Wyatt removed the tombs which had been fortuitously placed about the cathedral in the course of the centuries, and arranged them in two neat and precise lines between the pillars of the nave. In the carrying out of this work there was much wanton vandalism, destruction of beautiful tombs and disturbance of human remains; but once more Wyatt did succeed in restoring a clear, unified plan, with the result that today anyone looking up the cathedral from the west end or down from the High Altar obtains one single, grand, harmonious impression, which would certainly not have been obtainable before Wyatt carried out his work.

A further act for which Wyatt was responsible was the removal from the windows of the cathedral of the remainder of the beautiful thirteenth-century stained glass and the replacing of it with clear glazing. Here again Wyatt's objective was to let in sufficient light to enable the clarity and simplicity of the fundamental design to be apparent. It has to be remem-bered that thirteenth-century glass is usually dark in character, as is evident from the remains of the present Jesse window in the south nave aisle of the cathedral; and even the grisaille glass, of which most of the Salisbury glass consisted, is greenish-grey. This did not matter in medieval days when the whole of the cathedral was brightly painted and coloured; but in the eighteenth century, when all this colour had been removed through the Puritan influence of the two previous centuries, the cathedral must indeed have looked very dark and depressing with its ancient glass windows. None the less, the fact that Wyatt removed all this glass and had it broken up and thrown by the 'cartload' into the city ditches has justly earned him the censure of subsequent generations.

Again, Wyatt pulled down the old delicate and elegant medieval stone screen which divided the choir from the nave. (Part of this can now be seen on the west wall of the Morning Chapel.) In its place he erected a much larger, solid stone screen, mainly composed of fragments from the Hungerford and Beauchamp chantries, and placed the organ on top of it. This must be deeply regretted; but on the other hand it must be confessed that Wyatt's stone screen was a good piece of architectural workmanship, very different from the appalling Victorian monstrosity by which in the following century it was replaced. Finally, Wyatt removed the High Altar to the end of the Lady Chapel, thereby making both the cathedral and the chapel into one single unit. The High Altar was moved back into the sanctuary in Victorian times, but it was placed too far east, and the present reredos can only be regarded as a deplorable mistake. (Pl. 28)

Wyatt concluded by covering the whole of the interior with limewash, which may have made it somewhat lighter and cleaner, but was hardly a wise thing to do. How much of the responsibility for all this work rests with Wyatt and how much with the Bishop and the Dean and Chapter it is difficult to say; but it would appear that most of the drastic steps were taken at the express wish of the Bishop. It must also be remembered that Wyatt accomplished some valuable work of maintenance on the tower and spire and other parts of the cathedral; and although this was of a temporary character, he deserves credit for helping to preserve the building.

By 1792 the whole of the work of restoration was completed, and to do honour to the occasion 'on Friday morning, soon after eleven o'clock, the King and Queen, with the Princess Royal and the five other Princesses, Augusta, Elizabeth, Mary, Sophia, and Amelia . . . and a small retinue arrived at the Bishop's Palace. . . . After partaking of an elegant refection with the Bishop and his Lady, they visited the Cathedral Church, now quite finished, accompanied by the Bishop, the Dean and Chapter, several Prebendaries, the Earl of Pembroke, and Mr Wyatt, who attended to explain the several alterations and improvements, which their Majesties inspected with minute attention, and expressed much satisfaction not only at the elegance and propriety of each, but also at the boldly striking, yet simple and singularly beautiful effect of the *tout ensemble*. The Painted Window [the new East Window above the arch of the Lady Chapel] and the New Organ excited their particular notice. . . . The Coronation Anthem, Hallelujah from the *Messiah* and other pieces from Handel, to show the different stops, were excellently and judiciously performed by Mr. Corfe, the Organist, to the great gratification of his Royal Auditors'.

From the same source, the *Salisbury Journal*, can be gleaned the informa-tion that at the Musical Festival, in time for which the cathedral was reopened, the chorus and musicians rendered selections 'which consisted of every variety of the best music that could well be introduced in the course of five performances', and produced 'that awful and sublime effect which at once both pleased and astonished the numerous audience'. Indeed, the only fault or disturbance recorded was the interruption by a Quaker lady, who considered the whole thing 'rank idolatry', of Signora Storace's last cadence of 'I know that my Redeemer liveth', in which she was shining 'with peculiar excellence'.

While so much alteration was being carried out in the cathedral, changes occurred also in the city. In 1769 lamps and irons were provided for the streets; and in 1773 it is recorded that 'whereas about ten years ago there passed through the city, in the course of a week, from London to Exeter, six stage-coaches, each carrying six passengers, at present there constantly pass in the same time twenty-four coaches and twenty-eight stage-chaises, making on the whole 228 passengers' (Pl. 45). The travel boom had begun (Pl. 39).

A most important change in the buildings of the city resulted from the disastrous fire which in 1780 caused the destruction of the old Council House in the Market Square (Pl. 42). The customary banquet given by the new Mayor was given on the evening of 15 November, and at 5 a.m. next morning ('soon after the departure of the company') the upper storey of the building was found to be on fire. Help was promptly given, and the fire was extinguished by 9 a.m.; but irreparable damage had been done to the edifice. The story of its demolition belongs to the next chapter.

V

THE EXPANDING CITY

1790-1956

To WRITE A comprehensive history of Salisbury during the last century and a half is beyond the scope of this chapter. The closer we approach to the present day, the greater the mass of material available, and the more insuperable the difficulty of deciding which matters are likely to be of lasting historical importance. It has therefore seemed best to set certain limits to this study, and to attempt to build up a picture of the period from eight main viewpoints, looking at some changes in travel, trade and industry, local government, political movements, education, social life, religion, and finally architecture. Though the twentieth century is not ignored, the emphasis has been placed on the nineteenth. And if there is one key factor which emerges as a characteristic of the city at this time, it is 'expansion'.

John Halle, or any of his fifteenth-century contemporaries, would have had little difficulty in recognizing the Salisbury of 1660 or 1790; at first sight that of 1956 would have seemed to them at best a dream, at worst a fantastic nightmare. Such is the measure of the great changes this period brought about.

A closer look would have shown them many basic things still remaining in the heart of the city today (Pl. 44)—the cathedral itself and the Close surrounding it, altered in detail but still recognizable; the street pattern of the 'chequers', though without the characteristic canals; the churches and a sprinkling of houses familiar to them; the Tuesday market, the animals, and the produce sales. But what would they make of the change from a tiny medieval city of a few thousand souls to the busy market town of today and its sprawling spider's web of suburbs along all the main roads into the city—or of the change from the human bustle of their streets to the mechanical traffic jams of the modern market day?

Even such an unromantic source as the population census hides behind its dull exterior the index of a revolution. In the years from 1801 to 1891 the city's population more than doubled itself, from 7,832 to 15,890. In 1950 it was 33,000: in sixty years more than double again. Behind the change from the 865 heads in the parish of Fisherton in 1801 to the 4,783 in 1881 lies the growth and building of a suburb; the similar growth of Milford in the late nineteenth century, of Harnham, Castle Road, Bemerton Heath in the twentieth, mark the change more emphatically still.

One vital factor going to the making of this 'newer' Sarum was the development of easy and speedy methods of communication. Travel from medieval times to the seventeenth century was difficult and slow, not undertaken without good reason. The eighteenth century began the development of 'turnpike' roads, their construction and repair financed by public subscription and maintained by a proportion of the toll exacted from the traveller at the end of each stage of the road. By the end of the eighteenth century a number of these turnpikes led into Salisbury, and access to London, Southampton, Dorchester, and Exeter was possible by coach, wagon, or horseback.

But horse-drawn travel was slow and its loads limited; over a long journey it was expensive both in time and in passengers' accommodation and food *en route*. Something more was needed before there could be developed on the present scale the city's position as a centre of distribution for agriculture and light industry.

Towards the end of the eighteenth century came the project of opening the city to the sea by means of a canal to Southampton, and in 1793 a Bill was introduced into Parliament and a company set up for this purpose. The canal, according to Benson and Hatcher, was

to commence at the town of Southampton and taking the direction of Millbrook and Redbridge to join that of Andover. It was to diverge from the Andover Canal, at Kimbridge Mill, in the parish of Michael Marsh; and passing through Mottisfont, Lockerly, East and West Dean, the two Grimsteads, Alderbury, Petersfinger, Laverstock, and Milford, to terminate near the church of St Martin's at Salisbury.

The original capital of the company was to be £56,000. By 1798, when this capital had run out, the canal had been brought to Dean, and cuttings made as far as Alderbury (they can still be clearly seen today at, for instance, East Grimstead); but that, unfortunately, was the end. In spite of an appeal for further funds, and a local computation that on its completion the city would save £3,000 a year in the carriage of coals alone, no more money was forthcoming, and the scheme had to be abandoned. A later (1824) proposal to link Salisbury and Wilton to the Kennet and Avon Canal remained a proposal on paper. Not, perhaps, surprisingly, for in the following year Stephenson's steam locomotive opened the Stockton and Darlington Railway; and as the potentialities of this new method of travel were realized, there began all over England the 'railway fever' that was to open up the country as never before.

As early as 1831 local projects were being discussed, but the inaugural

26. The double-sided royal arms of the Georges from 1714 to 1801.
From a mayoral mace-stand in St Edmund's Church.

. Colonel Penruddock and his wife Arundell. The portrait of this sad couple still hangs at Compton
Park.

28. The interior of the cathedral in the eighteenth century, from a contemporary engraving. Renatus Harris's organ, removed by Wyatt, is lost, but he re-erected the screen in the Morning Chapel. The renaissance font is now in Yankalilla, South Australia.

29. The fire-place in the eighteenth-century Gothic room in Malmesbury House, Number 15 The Close, the former home of the Harris family.

o. The Palladian Bridge in Wilton Park, 1739. Ascribed to Henry, 9th Earl of Pembroke, and Roger Morris.

. The old Choristers' School, previously the Free School in the Close. There is no substantial evidence that it was designed by Wren.

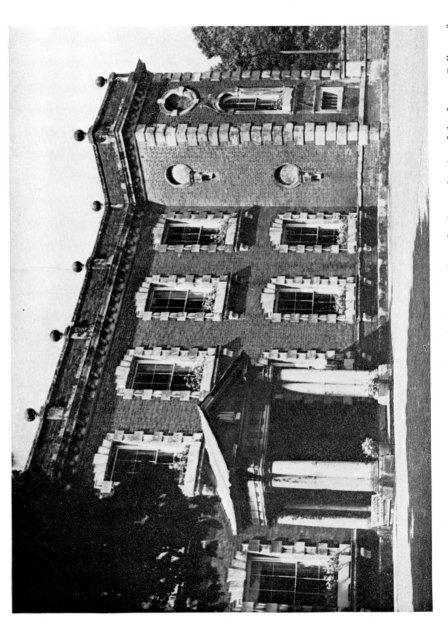

32. The present Council House, Bourne Hill. Rebuilt by the Wyndham family on the site of the former College of St Edmund.

33. Mompesson House, by the Choristers' Green, completed in 1701. Regarded as the most distinguished house in the Close.

34. The thirteenth-century bell tower in the cathedral churchyard. From Hatcher's *History of Salisbury*. Removed by Wyatt in 1789.

35. The Poultry Cross as 'repaired and beautified' in 1711. From an oil painting, *c.* 1850.
See plate 37

36. The vault of the chapter house. It is poised on a slender clustered shaft of Purbeck marble.

38. St Ann's Gate by night. Southwards from this gate the building of the embattled Close wall was begun by authority of Edward III.

37. The Poultry Cross today. As restored in the 1870's.
See plate 35

39. The White Hart Hotel. A former coaching inn.

40. The Council House as erected in 1795, now the Guild Hall. From a print in Salisbury Museum

41. Crimean Peace Banquet in the Market Place. The Giant, Hobnob, and Morris Men are in evidence
Lithograph, Salisbury Museum.

42. The Town House on fire, 1780, from a print in Salisbury Museum. The War Memorial now stands on the site in the Market Place.

3. Accident at I. K. Brunel's Fisherton Terminus, 1856. From a water-colour in Salisbury Museum.

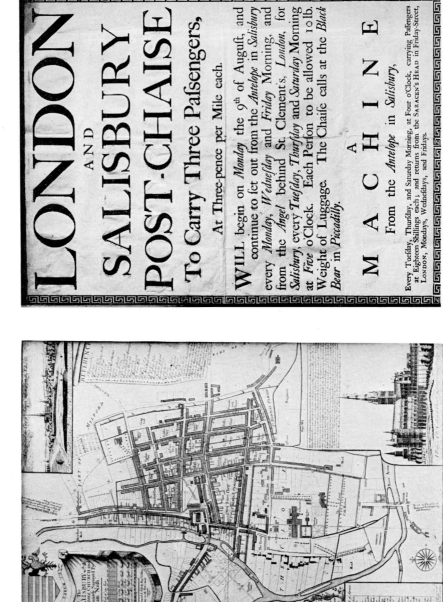

44. William Naish's map of Salisbury, 1751. Revised from an edition of 1726.

45. Post-chaise notice in Salisbury Museum.

LONDON
AND
SALISBURY
POST-CHAISE,
To Carry Three Paſſengers,
At Three-pence per Mile each.

WILL begin on *Monday* the 9th of Auguſt, and continue to ſet out from the *Antelope* in *Salisbury* every *Monday*, *Wedneſday* and *Friday* Morning, and from the *Angel* behind St. Clement's, *London*, for *Salisbury*, every *Tueſday*, *Thurſday* and *Saturday* Morning at *Five* o'Clock. Each Perſon to be allowed 10 lb. Weight of Luggage. The Chaiſe calls at the *Black Bear* in *Piccadilly*.

A
MACHINE
From the *Antelope* in *Salisbury*,

Every Tueſday, Thurſday, and Saturday Morning, at Four o'Clock, carrying Paſſengers at Eighteen Shillings each ; and returns from the SARACEN'S HEAD in Friday-Street, LONDON, Mondays, Wedneſdays, and Fridays.

46. Adam and Eve, from a carved frieze in the chapter house. One of a series of scenes from Old Testament history.

47. St Osmund's Church, designed by A. W. Pugin and later enlarged.

48. St Martin's Church School (Bothams and Brown, architects). Built in 1952 to replace the original school beside the church.

49. The Church of St Francis of Assisi (Robert Potter, architect), completed in 1940. The parish w
formed out of those of St Mark and Stratford-sub-Castle.

date for Salisbury was 27 January 1847, when the Salisbury and Bishop-stoke Railway was opened for goods traffic. At Bishopstoke junction—round which the new town of Eastleigh rapidly grew—it joined the already existing line to London, and when on 1 March the line was opened to passengers it became possible to travel from Salisbury to London in the unheard of time of four hours, less than half the time of the fastest coach. Henceforth there were to be four trains up and five down each day, and the return fare was 24s. 1st class, 18s. 6d. 2nd class. So popular was this innovation that, by 1850, excursion trains were being run to London for a fare of 3s. 6d. The Salisbury terminus was at the Milford station, largely a timber erection at that time; although the station is still in use for goods traffic, only one fragment of the original platform remains. The building which houses the mechanism of the weighbridge is the only survivor of the original structure.

The route *via* Eastleigh was of course an indirect one, but the opening in 1854 of the Basingstoke–Andover line brought the possibility of a more direct route to London; the Andover–Salisbury line in 1857 completed the link and brought the capital twelve miles nearer. At this stage the Milford station was still used, though its use was growing increasingly awkward. From the new line, the London trains now had to reverse into the station; adequate as a terminus, Milford would be con-siderably less than adequate if the line were extended west to Exeter. A fire in which the wooden station was severely damaged in 1858 accentuated the difficulties; and with the completion the following year of the tunnel, embankments, and the new bridge across Fisherton Street, a new 'Fisher-ton' station became the link on the line which now extended from London to Gillingham, and by 1860 was to reach Exeter. Milford then became, as it is today, a goods station.

Fisherton station at this time, of course, was much smaller than its present-day counterpart. The original main buildings are the present parcels offices; until 1901 the top storey remained the Station-master's house. These buildings were on the 'down' platform; the 'up' platform lay on the east side of Fisherton Bridge, with access from the street by stairs and an iron gate which, though long disused, can still be seen half hidden by an advertisement hoarding.

Meantime, as the line from London to the southwest was being extended, so was a further link between Salisbury and Bristol. On 30 June 1856 the Salisbury–Warminster Railway was opened, with a terminus also at Fisherton. This building, designed by Brunel, with its front facing on to Fisherton Street north of the bridge, still survives, though somewhat time-worn and neglected, its lines used now only for the unloading of merchandise.

It was this station, barely four months after its opening, that gave the citizens of Salisbury their first experience of a railway accident, fortunately with only two human casualties. A contemporary water-colour (Pl. 43)

I

preserved in the museum vividly records the scene, as also did the reporter of the *Salisbury and Winchester Journal*. It was a loaded cattle train from Bristol, pulled by two engines.

The train it seems passed Wilton at a rapid pace, and increased in speed after it had passed that station, and came with such violence into the terminus at Salisbury as to carry everything before it. The four sunken posts against which the buffers of the engine came in contact were broken off, and the floors and joists of the platform, as well as the walls of the ladies' waiting room, were as cleanly cut through as though it were the work of carpenters and masons. The outer wall was thrown down, and the first engine was parallel with the walls of the street. The hinder part of the first engine was resting on the front of the second, which from its great weight was embedded in the ground. The concussion threw the tender of the second engine on one end, and the first carriage being coupled thereto, was likewise forced up, and both were in a perpendicular position; the second carriage was almost in a similar position, and the third was entirely thrown over on to the fourth. The stoker of the first engine, on entering the station, jumped off on the platform, and struck his head, but otherwise was uninjured; the driver, Mays, however, kept his post, and was carried through to the street unhurt. It is almost impossible to describe the scene which ensued:—the gas was extinguished, fearing that some accident might accrue therefrom, and the only lights available were a few candles and dark lanterns; and the crowds of people which had assembled on the platform were tumbling over each other. The foremost engine emitted large volumes of steam, which filled the station, and rendered the little light less visible. Flames of fire were then discovered, which were caused by the timber of the floorings becoming ignited by the fire from the engine. The hose was immediately appended to the hydrants, and the plentiful supply of water therefrom, and that likewise thrown from buckets, soon extinguished the fire; had it been otherwise, in all probability the station would have been burnt to the ground. Everyone seemed panic-stricken; and all was dismay, confusion, perplexity, and darkness. Up to this time nothing had been done to remove the cattle, and the bodies of the unfortunate deceased had not been discovered. About half-past ten o'clock, steps were taken to extricate the sheep, and a very shocking spectacle they presented. Some few were alive, but many others were sadly torn and mangled; the majority were crushed to death, whilst some had their legs cut off or broken, and others' entrails were protruding. As soon as they were thrown out of the waggons, Messrs Judd and Dowding, Butchers of this city, at the request of the officials, slaughtered the injured, and dispatched them to be dressed. Whilst these operations were going on, the bodies of the engineer and stoker were found crushed between the tender and the firebox of the engine, the hand of the former only being visible; the latter was standing upright, and his face was all that could be observed. Every effort was immediately made to extricate them. . . .

Impressed as they were by the terror of the incident, the frugal Victorians still made quite sure that nothing would be wasted. . . .

Apart from comparatively minor accidents near Skew Bridge in 1873 and Downton in 1884, it was not till the summer of 1906 that Salisbury faced a serious railway accident, when an American boat special from Plymouth entered the Fisherton station too quickly, failed to take the curve, and hit an empty train standing alongside. Twenty-eight people were killed on that occasion; and for many years afterwards all trains on this line were compulsorily halted outside the station, to prevent a recurrence.

By the time of that accident, the railway plan of Salisbury had reached very nearly its present form. The Dorset line in 1866 had saved thirty-five miles on the journey to Poole; and in 1900–2 a large-scale reconstruction at Fisherton costing over £200,000 had united the two stations, created the marshalling sidings and engine sheds, and left the long 1,000-foot line of blank red-brick retaining wall that now dominates Churchfields and the old road to Bemerton.

In those fifty years the railways had speeded up communications within the district and with the rest of the country to a remarkable extent. It was left for the internal combustion engine in the twentieth century to complete the revolution.

Easier communications undoubtedly helped some trades in Salisbury, or brought others to the city. But they came too late to save the wool and weaving trade, to which the city owed its medieval prosperity. In the last quarter of the eighteenth century the trade still flourished—and it was as much an export as a home trade. Serges and flannels for Germany and the East Indies, coarse ('low') flannels for North America, fine flannels for pre-revolutionary France (the coloured under-waistcoats of King Louis's courtiers may well have been made from Salisbury cloth, and on at least one occasion Queen Charlotte wore a gown of fine Salisbury weave)—these were the standard fabrics; but there were also cloths with more romantic names—linseys, toilenettes, swan's-downs, or the 'marbled cloth' that was a kind of worsted, and the 'pepper and salt' for harder wear. The bulk of the raw wool came from the flocks of Wiltshire and Dorset; and something like a quarter of the city's population, under thirty or forty master manufacturers, seems to have been employed in the trade.

But the introduction of the spinning jenny (the first one appeared in the city in 1791) turned a small craft industry into a manufactory requiring power not easily available in Salisbury; the Revolutionary and Napoleonic Wars made trade with Europe difficult; the output of the large and increasing Yorkshire industry was more and more difficult to compete with; so that by 1843 Benson and Hatcher had regretfully to record that now 'the articles made here are too trifling to deserve notice'. The hardship and unemployment thus accelerated—in the countryside as well as in the city—find their echo not only in local attempts to provide Poor Relief, or in the machine wreckings and agricultural riots of the eighteen-thirties, but also in Hatcher's somewhat pathetic record of an early attempt at what the twentieth century might call a Development Area Scheme.

In 1825 an attempt was made to take advantage of the many resources which the city possesses for manufactures, by its central position, dense population, and command of water. Encouragement was offered, by advertisement, to any person who would suggest the means of furnishing occupation for the poor. This overture was so far successful, that a committee was appointed to enter into a treaty on the subject with a respectable manufacturer.

Unfortunately, like many another well-meant scheme, it seems to have got no further than a public meeting.

Another trade that had for centuries been associated with Salisbury and carried the city's reputation—that of the cutlers—was also to decline as the nineteenth century wore on. A couplet from a *Bath Guide* of the period runs:

> Let Bristol for commerce and dirt be renowned
> At Salisbury let penknives and scissors be ground,

and Easton, in his *Salisbury Guide*, as late as 1825 announces enthusias-tically:

The manufacture of cutlery is in this place brought to the highest degree of per-fection, and supposed infinitely to excel all others, the fine temperature [*sic*] of the steel being attributed to the peculiar quality of the water.

An old bill preserved in the museum records the infinite variety of the cutler's art. Apart from table cutlery there were scissors of all kinds—embroidery, nail and toilet, paper-hanging, draper's, garden, flower, vine, and haircutting; moustache and ordinary razors; pen- and pocket-knives, bread, cheese, and butcher's knives and steels, farrier's knives and fleams, sheep, potato, and sportsmen's knives; corkscrews, buttonhooks, pruning and budding knives, puzzle knives; cheese irons for tasting cheese; all craftsman's work, and owing nothing to the methods of mass production. But those very methods developed elsewhere were gradually to drive the master-cutler out of business. By 1839 Hearn in his *Guide to Salisbury* is much less enthusiastic than Easton. 'The cutler of Salisbury once maintained a considerable degree of celebrity, but notwithstanding the excellence of the article still manufactured here, it is now little known or patronized out of the district.'

Now the last of the company has departed; the shops are in other hands, the grindstones silent; and the Royal Arms that once gleamed over the door of a Salisbury Cutler survive only in a late eighteenth-century drawing.

While the traditional trades declined, others gradually took their place, for with unemployment and a still increasing population there was ample labour available. One such, which grew up in the latter half of the century, and in its turn disappeared, has left an architectural mark near the present omnibus station, in Endless Street. The building, with its pseudo-classical façade, is now a warehouse and shop; but carved in the stone parapet still remains the legend—INVICTA LEATHER WORKS— as a reminder of the factory that once stretched behind it into Rollestone Street, forming, as an article of 1897 put it, 'one of the chief industrial

FIG. 14. A grocer's warehouse, 24 The Canal

centres in Salisbury, and the largest leather currying business in the West of England, over one hundred hands finding constant employ, ment in the varying departments of the business. The history of the firm is one of rapid and substantial progress, and furnishes a striking illustration of what can be accomplished by skill, energy and enter, prise'. Less substantial, perhaps, and more evanescent than the writer of 1897 could envisage, but its mark remains on the city's face.

Another and more recent example of the attempts of modern industry to lay hold on the city belongs to the internal combustion age. A Salisbury firm of clock-makers at the turn of this century decided to manufacture the newly arrived motor-cycle. From that to the production of cars and commercial vehicles was a short step, and first in Friary Lane and subse, quently at the Excelsior Works in Bemerton, the early Scout Cars were produced. Only two are now known to the Veteran Car Club, but they played their part in the early development of motor transport. A photo, graph of one of them shows its adaptation to the needs of the countryside. In the early morning, its seats folded up, it was used for collecting milk, churns; then, after cleaning, the two long seats facing inwards on each side of the body were folded down, a strip of carpet was unrolled on the floor, and one of the earliest omnibuses was ready for its passengers.

By 1912 the peak production of two cars a week had been reached; but during the first world war production was suspended while the factory made munitions. After the war the car never recovered its early popularity, and though in 1922 the firm was still employing 150 men, shortly after that production was finally abandoned.

Although various forms of light engineering still flourish in the city, in spite of the great increase of population less than one in five of the city's workers is today engaged in industry. Salisbury in 1956 exists—as on a smaller scale it has done for over six hundred years—primarily as a trading centre and for the service it gives to the surrounding region and its people.

The expansion of the city created many new problems, and throughout the period local government was constantly being adapted and expanded in an attempt to cope with them. The first great change was brought about by the Municipal Reform Act of 1835, which removed many of the anachronisms still remaining from the medieval system of local government, and Salisbury withdrew the last remnants of temporal responsibility from the bishop. The boundaries of the city were extended and defined, and the old corporation became a new and more popularly elected city council. It is interesting to note that when this new council took office in 1836 it imposed a total rate for the borough of £469. The mayor's salary was to be £50, the town clerk's £70, and the treasurer's £10.

The new council was to acquire many new powers as the century wore on, and the city's boundaries were to be extended again in 1868, 1904, 1927, and 1954. One of the first of the new developments was the establishment and control, in the same year, 1836, of the first city police force. These men, modelled on Peel's London police, were 'to be clothed in a blue uniform, with the arms of Salisbury on one side of the collar, and the number on the other'. The force was to grow with the city. Its original headquarters was in The Canal, subsequently in Endless Street; the present building in the Wilton Road was built and opened in 1956.

But at the same time an effect of the Reform Bill of 1832 was to take away from the city some of its prerogatives. The division of the county into North and South Wiltshire had the effect of creating a second county town in Devizes, and attempts were immediately made to have the county assizes held there. This would be a blow not only to the city's prestige but also to its pocket, and a petition to the King was immediately drawn up, stating:

That this removal of the Assizes would create a needless expenditure of the public money; that it would produce a serious loss, and cause considerable depreciation in the value of property at Salisbury; it being calculated that £10,000 was annually expended in the City, in consequence of the concourse of people drawn together by the Assizes.

That the City, from its extent, and from the length of time the Assizes had been held here, possessed the requisite accommodations to a greater extent than any other place in the county.

That a convenient gaol had recently been built, in a suitable situation, and that the courts of justice had been enlarged and improved, not at the charge of the county, but by the voluntary contribution of the citizens themselves, to the amount of £3,500. That this alteration had been approved by the judges, magistrates, grand jury, barristers, and all other parties interested.

But the petition was only half availing; the Spring Assize was lost to the rival.

The gaol mentioned in the petition was the new gaol standing in Fisherton opposite St Paul's Church. This had been opened in 1822 to replace the former city gaol which had stood next the infirmary at Fisherton Bridge; the only surviving fragment of this building was incorporated in the foundations of the clock tower in 1893. The new gaol was used until 1869; part of the building is still standing. It had originally ninety-six cells, in seven courtyards, together with accommodation for debtors. The last execution took place there in 1855, the subject being one William Wright, found guilty of the murder of Ann Collins at Lydiard Tregoze near Swindon. It was a public execution, with the gallows set up at the junction of the Wilton and Devizes roads.

The scaffold was erected early on Tuesday morning, and shortly before eleven o'clock the culprit was attended in the chapel by the chaplain, who urged upon him with much earnestness the importance of properly employing the few moments he had to live. The Holy Sacrament was then administered, and at twenty minutes to twelve the mournful procession left the chapel. The unhappy man, who was accompanied by the chaplain, the under-sheriff, &c, walked with a firm step towards the fatal spot, the chaplain reading the service appointed by our church for the burial of the dead. On arriving at the press-room, the culprit appeared deeply affected; he sobbed violently, and engaged earnestly in prayer. He took his farewell of the governor, and shook hands with the chaplain and the under-sheriff. Calcraft the executioner then performed the process of pinioning; and as the miserable man had previously expressed his intention of addressing the crowd, he was asked if he still adhered to his determination? To this he replied in the negative, and the melancholy procession then ascended the steps leading to the scaffold. The culprit's firmness did not forsake him; and, having placed himself beneath the fatal beam, the rope was placed round his neck and adjusted, and the cap drawn over his eyes. The chaplain, with feelings of the deepest emotion, then proceeded with the solemn service, and at a given signal the bolt was drawn and the wretched man was launched into eternity. His death was almost instantaneous. The fall from the drop caused the wound which the unfortunate criminal inflicted upon himself at the time of the murder to break out afresh, and this tended considerably to increase the horror of the spectacle.

Eleven years later a Royal Commission was to recommend the abolition of public executions; no more scenes such as this were to be witnessed in the city.

Another form of public punishment, a minor form, though one that could be made exceedingly unpleasant if the public so desired—punishment in the stocks—was given up in 1858. The use of the pillory had been abolished in 1837. The pillory and stocks stood in the marketplace, and according to Northy:

to be pilloried was to suffer a greater punishment than many people may imagine, apart from the question of the disgrace. It was the common practice for the jeering rabble who assembled to pelt the hapless culprits with evilsmelling eggs, potatoes, turnips, and other missiles, often maiming the wretches for life, if not causing death.

The last offender to suffer the hazards of confinement in the stocks was John Selloway, charged in 1858 with being drunk.

This being the eighth charge of a similar nature against him during the last fourteen months, he was ordered to pay five shillings, or in default to be placed six hours in the stocks. The defendant refusing to pay the fine, the latter portion of the sentence was carried into effect.

The various courts of justice were held then, as now, in the Guild Hall in the market square (Pl. 40), at that time still known as the Council House. The old Council House had been greatly damaged by fire in 1780, as recorded in the previous chapter; and the then Earl of Radnor immediately offered to replace it at his own expense and to his own design. There was, however, some difficulty over this at first, since he suggested as the site for the new building the centre of the market square, and there were naturally many local objections raised. A solution was eventually reached by which the Dean and Chapter gave up the present site, that of the medieval guildhall, in exchange for some other property (including the old theatre at the Vine Inn) and by 1795 the new building was completed and handed over to the Mayor and Corporation. The old Town House was soon afterwards demolished. The letter from Lord Radnor handing over the new building is worth quoting as an example of the elaborate epistolary style of the period.

Camp near Folkestone Sept. 14 1795

Sir,

      The term has at last arrived when I can announce to you, and I do it with real pleasure, that my engagement entered on your minutes July 9th 1787, is performed. The new Council House is ready for your acceptance. I trust you will find it to your perfect satisfaction.

      Honoured as my family has been by you, upon various occasions and especially by the delegation of different individuals of it, during a period of more than half a century, without a single interruption, to represent your city in Parliament, a circumstance seldom paralleled in the annals of the kingdom, I am bound to deliver to you a monument of my respect, gratitude and attachment, which I believe to be without a parallel.

      If the genuine principles of loyalty—if the love of legal freedom—if the habitual observance of municipal decorum—if a manly sense of individual independence, shall migrate with you to your new Council House, and continue the characteristics of the members of this body, I shall, zealous as I am for your welfare, and sharing in your credit, have reason to be proud indeed.

It is an anxious wish of my heart that it may not, in after times, ever be suggested that with the remains of our homely but venerable building disappeared the simplicity of manners, the disinterestedness of conduct, the consistency of character of the citizens of Salisbury.

> I have the honour to be,
> With much respect and esteem,
> Your faithful and very obedient servant,
> RADNOR.

To the Mayor.

The building at that time differed from its present form in that a portico extended along the west side as well as the north. This was removed in 1889 when new cells had to be erected; while 'substantial and elegant' as the building had appeared to the eighteenth century, a hundred years later the Assize Courts were being described by one legal luminary as 'the worst in England'. Justified or not, the comment was taken to heart locally, and the extensive alterations of 1896–7 included the provision of a new Crown Court.

Measures to ensure public health were another responsibility the nineteenth century began to take more seriously than its predecessors. Insanitary conditions in a village or a small medieval town could be serious enough, as the periodical outbreaks of plague showed. But in a thickly populated and growing area their effects could be much more widespread. Moreover, men were becoming more and more conscious of methods by which illness could be prevented.

The matter was brought to a head in Salisbury by the outbreak of cholera in 1849. Between 8 July, when the first death was recorded, and 15 September, 160 people had died of cholera, and seventy-four from other causes closely allied to it. This was over six times the normal average death-rate for that time of the year, more than enough to shake the city out of any attitude of complacency. The November Thanksgiving services held in all the churches when the epidemic had abated were not the only evidences of the city's concern. The following year found complaints being registered regarding the deficiency of the city's drainage system. The 1848 Public Health Act was invoked, and in June 1851 a full-scale inquiry into the sanitary condition of the city was held by an inspector of the newly established Board of Health. His report, published in January 1852, surveyed the evidence put before the inquiry, and came to the following conclusions—conclusions which give us a clear picture of the state of affairs at this time:

That the comfort and health of the inhabitants would be promoted, and their condition improved, by—

(a) The drainage of the substratum of the city.
(b) A thorough system of surface drainage.

(c) A system of tubular drains for the removal of refuse, and adequate privy accommodation connected therewith.

(d) A sufficient supply of water of good quality.

(e) Improvement in the dwellings of the poor, particularly as regards ventilation.

(f) The removal of many nuisances, such as dung-heaps, offensive cess-pits, slaughter-houses, piggeries, &c.

(g) The better regulation of common lodging houses.

(h) Increased and improved lighting, particularly in Fisherton.

(i) The closing of the more crowded burial grounds within the city and the provision of extended burial accommodation in quarters more removed from the dwelling of the inhabitants.

The Public Health Act of 1848 should accordingly be applied to the borough, the City Council becoming the local Board of Health for the district.

These recommendations were all put into effect, some almost immediately, some over a longer period. The most immediate was the provision of a water-works and water-supply, and enclosed drainage for the whole city. This was completed by 1854, at a cost of some £27,000, and was followed by a gradual closing of the open channels and ditches which had hitherto run down each street and been the city's drainage system since medieval times. (There were still those in 1852 who argued against the new scheme on the grounds that the open system was quite adequate.) By 1860 the closure was practically complete, and another link with the Middle Ages had gone. The closing of the burial grounds and the opening of the new cemetery came in 1857.

Lighting and road maintenance had not always been a formal local government responsibility. As late as February 1812, for instance, we find a public meeting being called 'to consider of means for better lighting, paving, and watching the City. A subscription was raised for the purpose, and our venerable representative Mr Hussey set a liberal example, by offering no less a sum than £1,000 as his contribution'.

(Mr Hussey was indeed venerable; he died the following year aged eighty-seven, having been Member of Parliament for the city for thirty-nine years.)

On 10 January 1833 street lighting by gas was first introduced—again not without some opposition. 'Many were the forebodings of the evils that would result from its use, suffocation and poisoning, explosion and conflagration, being among the terrors dreaded by the more nervous of those who looked upon the innovation with disfavour.' However, their fears were soon dispelled, and the gas did its duty until, at the end of the century, it was replaced by electricity.

Not a little of the road improvement undertaken in the city during the nineteenth century was done as a form of poor relief. In 1816, for instance, 'Great privations and difficulties having been felt among the poorer classes, in consequence of the want of employment, a liberal subscription was raised in the city to turn their labour to some beneficial purpose. It amounted to no less than £1,327. They were first employed in digging gravel and repairing the streets; and afterwards in cutting down part of the road over Harnham Hill.' In 1817 the work was continued. Similar relief work was to be undertaken in the eighties and nineties on Milford Way.

Periodically, too, relief funds were to be set up to assist the poorer victims of the climate—usually snow or the flooding which followed it: the years 1836, 1841, and 1883 were typical examples. In the last year the flood damage at Fisherton was estimated at about £2,000, a considerable amount for those days. Wheeler's brief account of the 1841 flood (com- memorated still for the traveller of today by wall plaques on some of the cottages in those villages of Salisbury Plain which suffered most) gives a glimpse of the prevailing conditions.

On Saturday evening, the 16th January, the city was subjected to the most rapid inundation that had been known for many years, caused by a sudden thaw at a time the ground was so deeply frozen that none of the water could be absorbed. On Sunday morning the south-western portion of the Close was an unbroken sheet of water, extending to the doors of the Cathedral, so that Divine Service could not be performed. At West Harnham a cottage was washed away, the inhabitants having barely time to escape; the bridge at Laverstock was washed down, a man named Collins losing his life in attempting to draw the hatches. Fisherton was impassable on foot for two days. Part of the park wall at Wilton was washed away, several pigs were drowned, and the stabling at the George at Wishford was destroyed; but it was at Shrewton and the neighbouring villages that the greatest mischief was done; the water rose to a height of four or five feet, and many cottages were washed away, and three lives lost. In Shrewton, Maddington, the Orchestons, and Winterbourne Stoke, 63 cottages were destroyed and about 200 persons rendered homeless. A subscription was set on foot, and some £4,000 raised for the relief of the sufferers.

The foundation of another form of social welfare, the city's various almshouses, has been described in Chapter IV. The last to be founded, Hussey's Almshouses, came in 1794. They consisted of thirteen cottages in Castle Street, each endowed with 3s. 6d. per week. A number of the older foundations, however, owe their present appearance to the nine- teenth century. Blechynden's Almshouses in Winchester Street were rebuilt in 1857, Eyre's in 1872, Hussey's in 1875, Taylor's in 1886, and Brickett's in 1895.

In 1891 one of the inspectors of the Charity Commission held an inquiry into the various municipal charities, and in 1892 a new scheme for their more efficient administration was adopted. The medieval foundation, St Nicholas's Hospital, had come under review somewhat earlier, at an inquiry in 1883. St Nicholas's is sometimes said to have provided the Victorian novelist Anthony Trollope with the setting and some of the material for his novel *The Warden*, though claims have also been staked for Winchester. Certain it is—on Trollope's own authority— that it was in Salisbury that the story was conceived. In the course of his official duties at the G.P.O. on the organization of rural postal services, Trollope was in the city in 1851. In his autobiography he writes:

while wandering there one mid-summer evening round the purlieus of the cathedral I conceived the story of *The Warden*—from whence came that series of novels of which Barchester, with its bishops, deans and archdeacon, was the central site. . . . On the 29th of July 1852 . . . I began *The Warden*, at Tenbury, in Worcestershire. It was then more than twelve months since I had stood for an hour on the little bridge in Salisbury, and had made out to my own satisfaction the spot on which Hiram's Hospital should stand.

The Barchester novels are imaginative works, but no doubt something of the atmosphere of the city in Victorian times has found its way into their pages.

The relief of poverty and unemployment, during the early part of the century at least, was much too great a task for the old-established charities, or spasmodic private subscription. The New Poor Law of 1834 imposed the 'workhouse test' on all applicants for public alms. Every 'union' of parishes was to have a workhouse, administered by locally elected Boards of Guardians of the Poor, and the principle they were to adopt was the need to make life in the workhouse less attractive than the meanest kind of employment outside. Readers of Dickens's *Oliver Twist* will have no difficulty in visualizing what this could mean. The workhouse of the Alderbury Union was built at the junction of the Blandford and Odstock road, to the south of the city, and, as might be expected, it had its periods of storm. In 1881, for instance, the tower which has now given the build-ing a new name became the refuge of the women and children during a riot which caused a good deal of damage—and had its logical sequel at the next Quarter Sessions.

The city infirmary, which had been founded in 1766, continued to develop throughout the period. Its president from 1842 to 1861 was Sidney Herbert, Lord Herbert of Lea, whose memorial statue stood for many years in the Guildhall square, until its recent removal to the Vic-toria Park. His long friendship with Miss Florence Nightingale brought her influence to bear on the work of the hospital, and on more than one occasion she gave advice and made suggestions which the committee adopted. The infirmary was supported by voluntary contributions, and its administrators were frequently preoccupied with financial problems until in 1946 it became part of the National Health Service.

As in any other nineteenth-century town we find echoes in Salisbury of the various economic and political movements of the time. In the first half of the century in particular, the high level of unemployment among the poorer groups, already discussed, and the poverty and depression in the agricultural areas, led to a good deal of unrest. The so-called 'Speenham-land System' had provided for the subsidizing of the labourer's inadequate wages out of the rates—thus in effect encouraging farmers to refuse any increase in wages, and compelling the labourer to become a pauper even when in full work. The moral effect was bad on both sides. The increasing enclosure of open fields and commons, the decline of cottage industries, and the absence in this part of the country of any alternative employment, made the village labourer's position seem almost hopeless. Agitation began for a minimum wage in the winter of 10s. per week, in the summer of 12s. As elsewhere, some of the blame for the prevailing conditions was laid on the new machines coming into use, and incendiarism and machinewrecking parties became more and more common. By the end of November 1830 more widespread violence was threatened. It was reported that parties of labourers were collecting in different quarters, and one group, armed with bludgeons, crowbars, and pieces of machinery, fresh from destroying a threshing machine on Bishopsdown Farm, was marching on the city to destroy Figes's Iron Foundry. Wadham Wyndham, one of the city's Members of Parliament and a local magistrate,

placing himself at the head of a body of special constables, met them by the Green Croft, and having vainly expostulated with them, the Riot Act was read, and the mob, charged by the Yeomanry, were driven on to the high ground where St Edmund's Rectory now stands, and dispersed, twentytwo being taken into custody, and the remainder disarmed. . . . The Hindon Troop arrived next day, and scoured the country, dispersing the assemblages or taking them into custody. In the neighbourhood of Tisbury and other parts, the Yeomanry were sorely tried, and were ultimately obliged to charge the rioters, several on both sides being wounded, and near Pyt House one man was killed. At West Park, Mr Eyre Coote and a party of ten were attacked by the rioters, led by Cooper, son of a farmer of Grimstead, the struggle lasting the whole night. They were relieved by the Yeomanry in the morning, having previously captured ten of the mob.

Gradually quiet was restored, but the trouble had been widespread over most of the counties south of the Thames, as well as locally. At a special assize afterwards there were 332 prisoners for trial, twentyeight of whom were sentenced to transportation for life. One of the sequels in Salisbury was the strengthening of the Yeomanry and the formation of a new body of volunteer infantry who would be armed by the government, but would be unpaid, would find their own uniforms, and would not be called upon to serve more than three miles from Salisbury. A further sequel was that, in some areas at least, conditions for the agricultural labourer were somewhat improved.

This was the period, too, when there was considerable agitation for Parliamentary reform. Parliamentary representation, unchanged for centuries, had failed to keep pace with shifts of population. Huge centres of population like Manchester and Birmingham had no representation at all, while some sixty 'rotten boroughs' (as Cobbett called them), with little or no population, continued to return their traditional two members. Of these, Old Sarum was the classic example.

By this time it had become, as it is today, completely deserted, 'only a green mound without a habitation upon it'. The electoral procedure was this. Shortly before an election was due, the Lord of the Manor granted leases of 'burgage tenements' to two people, who then became the 'electors' for the time being. Having then 'voted' for the Lord's two nominees (usually in a tent set up under an elm-tree, known locally as 'Parliament-Tree') they quietly gave up their leases, and nothing more was heard of them or their successors till the next election.

The struggle, before the Bill to amend this and other electoral anomalies was finally passed, is a matter of national history, but it was keenly followed and debated locally, and eventually its success was celebrated on 26 and 27 June 1832, by great illuminations in the city, processions, and a public dinner in which 2,600 people took part. More will be said later of the city's gargantuan feasts and celebrations.

A further attempt at electoral reform found an echo in the city in 1866, when Mr Gladstone and his family had come down to stay with an old friend of his, Bishop Hamilton. Gladstone had recently introduced a Bill to empower the further redistribution of some fifty constituencies. This had been rejected in committee, and the Liberal government, of which he was then Chancellor of the Exchequer, resigned. There had been demon-strations all over the country in favour of the reform; in Salisbury the local Liberals took the opportunity to stage a packed meeting, at which a congratulatory address was presented.

To the Right Hon. W. E. Gladstone, M.P.

Sir,

We, the Liberal electors and non-electors of the city of Salisbury, gladly embrace the opportunity of your visit to our ancient city to address you in testimony of our respect for your personal character, and of admiration for your public career.

We desire to tender our earnest thanks to you for many national benefits that have accrued from your management of the financial affairs of this great country, and we trust that ere long the power of inaugurating further fiscal improvement may again be in your hands.

We also beg to express our profound regret that the course of action pursued by a section of the Liberal party in the past session of Parliament has led to the overthrow of the judicious measure of Reform introduced by you, and which, having justice for its basis, we believe to be essential to the welfare of the community.

We cherish the conviction that the country is ripe for action in this matter, and that the next session must witness a Liberal Government dealing satisfactorily with the question.

We trust that your life may long be spared and that this country may continue to have the advantage of your great abilities, and of your undoubted political honesty.

What Mr Gladstone said on that occasion is preserved in some 4,500 words of the *Salisbury Journal* of the time. Ironically, the Reform Bill was later put through by the other political party.

The local newspapers of the nineteenth century allotted a good deal of their space to speeches and oratory, and the detail of the reporting is remarkable by modern standards. In 1843, for example, when during the Anti-Corn Law agitation Bright and Cobden came to the city to address a crowd of some 4,000 people assembled on the Green Croft, the report of that meeting, and of the speeches at a dinner of a hundred gentlemen at the Assembly Rooms which followed it, occupies over five closely printed columns, a matter of some 12,000 words, and nearly a quarter of the contents of the whole paper. One may perhaps be pardoned for detecting a certain air of protest from the reporter who, not yet half-way through his marathon, is faced not only with fecundity of phrase, but also with repetition. John Bright had just sat down, after making a long speech. 'The chairman then introduced Mr Cobden M.P. to the meeting. He was enthusiastically received, and delivered an able and amusing speech, which was in some particulars strikingly similar to the one addressed to the farmers at Winchester, a report of which appeared in a recent Journal. . . .' There follow some 5,000 words of his speech!

The present system of education in England, both voluntary and state, is largely a product of the nineteenth and twentieth centuries, and the developments that can be traced in the city form an epitome of the changes in popular education in the country as a whole. Beginning as a philan-thropic attempt to ameliorate the condition of the poor by opening up new avenues of employment, encouraging thrift, and inculcating the virtues of self-help, it was to end with a complete national system of primary, secondary, technical, university, and further education.

In the development of elementary education the city was to take part in the various voluntary movements that preceded the state system; and during the nineteenth-century controversy as to whether education should be religious or secular in its outlook, the church gave a lead to ensure that, in Salisbury, at least, the main influence was to be religious.

Sunday schools and ragged schools played an early part in this move-ment, and as early as 1811, in the parish of St Martin's, one of 'Bell's National Schools' was established (Pl. 48). Dr Bell, who was at one time Rector of Swanage, had while in charge of an orphan asylum at Madras evolved a monitorial method of education by which the older children were made to teach the younger ones, so that one master could supervise the work of a whole school. This 'Madras system', as it came to be called, made religious instruction an essential part of the plan, whose ultimate object, in Bell's own words, was 'to make good scholars, good men, good subjects, and good Christians; in other words, to promote the temporal and spiritual welfare of our pupils'.

As such, it was the system adopted by 'The National Society for Promoting the Education of the Poor in the Principles of the Established Church in England and Wales', a national voluntary body which sponsored and helped by grant-aid the establishment of schools in various parts of the country. After St Martin's other schools were to follow, and buildings to be erected, for the steadily increasing population made the need for them ever more insistent. The new schools in St Edmund's Parish were opened in 1860, St Thomas's in 1863, the Fisherton Schools in 1868, and the new Free School in Milford Street in 1873. A contemporary description of the latter, a school for 260 children built at a cost of £1,500, indicates the kind of premises that at this time were considered adequate. The bulk of the classes, of all ages, met in one or two large rooms, for ease of supervision.

The building, which is late Gothic in style, is built of brick, with stone dressings. It consists of a boys' school on the ground floor (43 feet long by 19 feet wide, and 14 feet high), a classroom, and lavatory, with an entrance lobby. In the upper part of the building is the girls' schoolroom, which is of similar dimensions to that below, having an open roof, ceiled at the level of the collar beams. There is also a classroom, together with a lavatory. Behind the schoolroom are commodious playrooms for both boys and girls. . . .

Less commodious to the modern eye, and probably recognized by few nowadays, this building still exists, no longer a school, but used as the premises of a dyeing and cleaning firm.

To help in the supply of teachers for these schools, the Diocese in 1841 opened a training college for schoolmistresses in King's House, in the Close. Something of the life of these girls at the time may be gathered from Hardy's novel *Jude the Obscure*, whose heroine was a student there. Now expanded out of all recognition, the Diocesan Training College has a national reputation, and its new buildings have, not without controversy, recently provided a flash of modernity in the architecture of the Close.

The voluntary movements were inadequate for the growing need, however, and the Elementary Education Act of 1870 provided that where educational facilities were insufficient and the religious denominations unable to provide them, School Boards were to be set up with rating powers to establish and maintain public elementary schools, and to compel the attendance of children between the ages of five and thirteen. School Boards might also be set up at once at the request of the ratepayers, and the existing voluntary schools transferred to their charge. As might be expected this proposal caused a good deal of controversy locally. Meetings were held to consider the position, and in February one of the city's distinguished educationalists and Liberal politicians, Henry Fawcett, Professor of Political Economy at Cambridge and a member of Gladstone's cabinet (his memorial statue is still in the Market Square), came down to lecture on 'The Education Question'. Fawcett had been blinded as a young man by a shooting accident on Harnham Hill, but in spite of his disability had achieved a distinguished academic and political career, and his popularity was high. How far this or his eloquence swayed local opinion is impossible at this stage to estimate, but in December the City

Council applied to the Board of Education to establish a local School Board, and in February 1871 that board was elected. Thus a further responsibility was to be added to the city, which it was not to lose until the Education Act of 1944 transferred many of its powers to the County Council. Controversy over Voluntary or Board schools did not die down with the formation of the School Board, however, but was to flare up from time to time for many years afterwards.

Though provision was now being made for elementary education, secondary education in the city had almost disappeared. There had been two old-established grammar-schools, one in the Close and one in the city, and while during the eighteenth century particularly they had flourished, they had now fallen on evil days. The school in the Close had almost petered out, and become solely the Choristers' School. It was later to achieve a renaissance and become a preparatory school, the Cathedral School of today. The city foundation was in an even worse state. A public investigation in 1855 revealed that the office of Master was almost a complete sinecure; that the reverend gentleman who then held the office had held it since 1804, had never had more than twenty-two pupils, and at that time had only seven; and that he did not often bother to turn up to instruct those he had.

This gap was not filled until 1889, and then largely owing to the initiative and inspiration of the then Bishop, John Wordsworth. As part of a scheme of expansion of the Church Day School Association, the George Herbert School in Gigant Street, St Mark's, Fisherton, and an extension at St Thomas's school were all to be opened in 1890. The Bishop decided to found at the same time a 'Higher Grade Elementary School', as the title then was; and first in his own palace, and subsequently in the buildings in Exeter Street, took shape the grammar-school now well known as Bishop Wordsworth's School. At the same time an older foundation, the Godolphin School for Girls, was expanding rapidly and soon became a girls' public school. Not till 1927 was the foundation of the Salisbury and South Wilts Grammar School to illustrate fully the passing of responsibility and patronage in this field to a public body, the Wiltshire Education Authority.

Further Education, as it is known today, was also represented in the city's development. As early as 1833 the movement inspired nationally by Dr Birkbeck took root here, and a Mechanics' Institute was formed, meeting in rooms in Salt Lane. A further impetus in the middle of the century, probably owing not a little to the interest in science and engineering aroused by the preparation of the Great Exhibition of 1851 (Salisbury was to have its own small exhibition the following year), brought the foundation in 1850 of the Literary and Scientific Institute. Neither of these bodies was adequately or permanently housed. It was left for their successor, the Literary Institute and School of Science and Art, founded in 1865, to acquire a set of new buildings, the premises in New Street

K

which were built in 1871 and now form the city's School of Art and Crafts. Important and valuable as these buildings have been education, ally, it remains a matter of regret to the historian that their ugly façade, in the worst style of the Victorian utility-gothic, could be achieved only at the expense of pulling down the Georgian theatre which had previously occupied the site.

Another important national movement, out of which, in the larger centres of population, were to grow the new universities, reached Salisbury in February and March 1886, when Professor Pulling of the Yorkshire College, Leeds (later to become Leeds University), gave a series of twelve University Extension lectures, inaugurating a tradition of University Adult Education in the city which still continues. The distinctive contribution of the twentieth century has been the College of Further Education, still temporarily housed, but developing rapidly as a centre of vocational training.

The present age appears largely to take for granted such well-used institutions as the City Public Library and the Museum in St Ann Street, yet these, too, we owe to the nineteenth century. The earliest attempt at a library was in 1816, when a number of citizens founded the Salisbury and South Wilts Library and Reading Society; but it was not till 1890 that the present Public Library maintained by the ratepayers was established, and then not without considerable opposition. After much argument the final decision was left to a public ballot; the result, 984 votes for, 856 against, shows how easily the decision might have gone the other way. On 16 December of that year the new library was opened, its first premises in part of the old Congregational Chapel in Endless Street. In 1905, and with the aid of £4,000 from the Carnegie Trust, the present building in Chipper Lane was erected; the Young Gallery was added by private benefaction five years later.

The Salisbury, South Wilts, and Blackmore Museum, as its full name suggests, had a dual origin. During the eighteenth century, particularly, an interest in local antiquities had become a hobby of many of the country gentry, and an area so full of prehistoric sites as this provided ample opportunity for the amateur archaeologist. Some valuable dis, coveries were made, and some irreparable damage done. No attempt, however, was made to form a local collection, available to the public, until the middle of the nineteenth century. At that time (1852), as already noted, the city's canals were being filled in, and many interesting relics were coming to light in the process. Dr Richard Fowler, a local antiquary and Fellow of the Royal Society, a man deeply interested in both history and education (he also founded the Working Men's Institute in St Ann Street), conceived the idea of collecting and displaying all the 'Drainage Collection' under one roof. A committee raised the necessary funds, and in June 1861, in rooms adjoining the Market House in Castle Street, the first collection was shown. In January 1864 the permanent home in St Ann Street was formally opened and additional material added. At the same time a separate building behind it was being erected to house the collection of primitive implements from prehistoric European and American sources formed by William Blackmore. This was opened three years later; and for nearly forty years the two museums continued to develop side by side, closely connected in practice, though in fact two separate establishments. In 1904 they were united, and since then, in spite of periodical financial crises, for there were few endowments, the joint museum has continued to expand and to acquire a character all its own. To quote Frank Stevens, a descendant of one of the founders, and for many years its able director: 'The Salisbury Museum is a distinctive local product, founded by local men, and directed by local antiquaries. Its galleries have been built by local residents . . . and filled with specimens mainly collected by local excavators.' The quality of many of its exhibits is high; some are unique; and now in the middle of the twentieth century the city may well be proud of its own museum.

One of the most impressive exhibits contained in the museum is the giant effigy of St Christopher, and his attendant 'Hob-Nob'. Relics of the pageantry of the medieval guilds, they still make public appearances in the streets on rare ceremonial occasions, attended by a group of morris dancers. One such occasion was on 28 June 1838, for the coronation of Queen Victoria, when a contemporary tells us:

The day was not allowed to grow very old before the spirit of gaiety was abroad in the ancient streets, and by ten o'clock the carrying out of the pre-arranged plan was begun. At that hour there was a parade of 300 Sunday School children, and shortly afterwards the strains of martial music were heard, and the Salisbury Troop of Yeomanry marched through the town *en route* to their training ground on the Race Plain. Sometime subsequently the Yeomanry returned and joined the Volunteers in a parade through the streets, through which also wended a procession of which our familiar friends the Giant and Hobnob were conspicuous figures. Such an auspicious event could not, of course, pass off without the feasting so dear still to the heart of an Englishman worth the name. Accordingly the Mayor and Corporation, with the magistrates, charitable trustees, and officers of Yeomanry and Volunteers, sat down at the Council Chamber to a sumptuous banquet—to which Mr Sidney Herbert contributed a fine buck—supplied by Clapperton of the Three Swans. The members of the volunteer corps dined at their headquarters; meals of a less formal kind were held at many of the inns, whilst there were also feasting and rejoicing in most of the houses in the old city. Mr J. Naish of the White Horse Inn in Castle street, roasted a sheep whole outside his premises, and a similar event took place in Fisherton street.

Comforts were distributed to the poor, amusements provided on the Green Croft, and the day ended with a great firework display.

There were other occasions for celebrations which were not neglected— as when Lord Nelson was given the freedom of the city in 1800, or the peace celebrations for the end of the Napoleonic Wars in 1814, when two fat sheep and an ox were roasted whole in the Market Place. In 1855, not without a good deal of unexpected comedy, as the local newspapers record, a great bonfire celebrated the fall of Sebastopol, and a year later the end of the Crimean War brought another Market Place feast (Pl. 41). (It was in 1858 that the 'Sebastopol gun' was mounted in the square, to remain there till removed and melted down for scrap-metal in the war of 1939–45.) There were royal visits, too—George III in 1792, the Prince Consort in 1851 (no doubt he gave advice on the city's proposed exhibi- tion the following year), and in 1856 the Queen herself and her family, on their way to Osborne in the Isle of Wight.

In 1887, however, for Her Majesty's Jubilee, the city surpassed itself. A large bonfire was lit on Harnham Hill on the eve of the Jubilee. On the day itself, crowds assembled early 'bent on the enjoyment which fell to their lot, and with which [sic] only the too potent rays of the brilliant midsummer sun lent anything like inconvenience'.

A procession, a service in the cathedral, another procession, and then, in the Market Place, the climax. 'Here dinner was served at long tables, placed in the open square. Between 3,000 and 4,000 men sat down, and their wants were ministered to by a staff of no less than 400 carvers. Grace was said by the Dean, and then the great company "set to", and the grand old Market Place echoed with the sound of cutlery, the chinking of glasses, and the merry chatter of the diners. . . . On the proposal of his worship [the Mayor] the Queen's health was drunk with much en- thusiasm, and when the band afterwards struck up the air of the National Anthem, the strain was heartily sung by nearly 4,000 throats.'

Nor was this all. The Mayor, Mr Griffin, had led the movement for the provision of an adequate recreation ground in the city, and afterwards, with great ceremony and 'rustic sports, witnessed by some 10,000 people', what is now known as the Victoria Park was opened. Altogether 1887 was an eventful year for the city; the Bath and West of England Agri- cultural Show, a visit from the Royal Archaeological Institute, a great Choral Festival in the cathedral, and in November a Guy Fawkes demonstration by the 'Bonfire Boys', helped to make the year memorable. A more permanent memorial (in addition to the park) was the planting of the trees which still grace the Market Square.

The Victoria Park was to provide in time many valuable facilities for sport—football, athletics, tennis, bowls. Some years earlier, 26–8 June 1854, the city had its first important cricket match, when South Wiltshire met All-England, and managed to win by three runs. Admittedly the Wiltshiremen played sixteen men and two professionals against the normal eleven; but All-England had the great Kent amateur Alfred Mynn, who even at the age of forty-seven was worth several ordinary players. But to have seen Mynn playing and to have beaten the visitors by so narrow a margin must have made a memorable match for the local spectators. Another was held the next year, and again in 1859; but on that occasion, even with eighteen men to All-England's eleven South Wiltshire was beaten by an innings and twenty-three runs!

Another periodical source of spectacular entertainment sprang from the area's growing importance as a centre for military training. Manœuvres and exercises had of course been held here for many years, but they were now growing in scale. The autumn manœuvres of 1872 brought the Prince of Wales to the city as a spectator, and on 12 September at the foot of Beacon Hill (which formed an admirable stand for spectators) was held a great march past of the troops. One of those present records in the pompous style of the period:

By ten o'clock a vast concourse of people had assembled in the neighbourhood of Beacon Hill, and by the time fixed for the review at noon it is calculated that there were about 10,0000 lookers-on at this grand military display. At 12 o'clock the royal salute boomed from a battery of artillery, announcing the arrival of the Prince of Wales, who was received by the Duke of Cambridge, a large staff of general officers, and the foreign military representatives. Needless to say His Royal Highness was received with a veritable roar of enthusiasm from the lungs and throats of loyal Wilt-shiremen and other patriotic people. Among the spectators was a distinguished company. . . . The march past commenced about 1.30, and lasted an hour and forty minutes, during which time the vast concourse of people were enabled to feast their eyes on a scene of stirring martial brilliancy and magnificence. Among the troops taking part were the Wilts Yeomanry, whose soldier-like bearing drew expressions of appreciation from the crowd.

Bernard Shaw's *Arms and the Man* had not yet burst on a startled Victorian world.

When in 1897 the government purchased some sixty square miles of Salisbury Plain at a cost of £450,000 for use as a military training area, it was clear that this influence on the city's life was to become permanent.

The artistic life of Salisbury, so prominent in the eighteenth century, was also to continue throughout the later period, though perhaps not at such a high level. Yet with regular choral festivals, and the Philharmonic Society established in 1839, there was music in plenty, and from time to time outstanding visiting artists. In 1846 the Abbé Liszt played at the Assembly Rooms; ten years later Jenny Lind sang there. Ole Bull, Thalberg, and Carlotta Patti were other artists who made periodical visits. In mid century there were occasional exhibitions of painting. Holman Hunt's 'The Light of the World' and 'Christ in the Temple' were on view in 1861 and 1864; Frith's 'Railway Station' in 1863. The city appears to have been spared the impact of 'Derby Day'.

In the early part of the nineteenth century the impetus which during Georgian and Regency days had made the theatre in New Street such an important part of Salisbury life during the winter began to die down. While James Shatford, who had taken control of the theatre and company in 1790, was still alive, affairs prospered, but after his death in 1809 the decline set in. His wife carried on the management for some years, but

Mrs Shatford, a fellow player tells us, was 'penny wise and pound foolish'. Moreover, the end of the Napoleonic Wars caused a considerable reduction in the numbers of troops stationed in the neighbourhood, and they had always been regular supporters of the playhouse. For some years guest artists from London, playing for short seasons with the stock company, were an attraction; Foot, Elliston, Kean, Dowton were among those who appeared with success in this way. Macready's visit in 1835 seems to have been less successful, at any rate from his own point of view.

My Lady Macbeth was a relic of a style gone by, the veritable 'ti⁄tum⁄to' 'jerk and duck and twist' in a most engaging manner. Tried to act Macbeth, but 'confusion to my lady!' it was too farcical, and would have been good as Dollalolla, but quite a travesty in the part she played. Nearly betrayed on one occasion my anger at one of the performers, but was very thankful that I subdued it before an opportunity for explosion was given; most happily I did not expose myself. The end of the play found me very much exhausted.

And though on the next night he felt he acted Hamlet 'remarkably well', at the next performance he 'acted Werner but middlingly; was harassed and disconcerted occasionally by the performers, and disturbed by various rioters in the course of the performance'. Altogether, not a happy three days; but the conditions were impossible.

Perhaps the most popular visitor at this period was John Vandenhoff, who was not only a well⁄known London actor but also a Salisbury man, having been born in Castle Street, and making his first stage appearance in the city on 11 May 1808, playing Osmund in the popular melodrama *The Castle Spectre* (written by Matthew 'Monk' Lewis, sometime M.P. for Hindon). Subsequently, Vandenhoff built up a national reputation, and over the years (except when touring in America) he made regular visits to Salisbury, where the local boy who had made good was always well received. He made his last appearance on the Salisbury stage in April 1856, only five years before his death.

Eventually the New Street theatre was closed, and pulled down to make way for the School of Science and Art. Thus it was to the Assembly Rooms or the Hamilton Hall in the Art School that in the sixties, seventies, and eighties came Charles Mathews, J. L. Toole, German Reed, and Corney Grain, Charles Hawtrey, and the D'Oyly Carte companies with the new operas by Gilbert and Sullivan. The lack of a regular theatre was soon felt. By 1888 arrangements had been made to begin building a new theatre in Chipper Lane and Endless Street—the County Hall. It was designed 'to accommodate 1,000 persons in all, with a stage 30 feet by 48 feet capable of holding 175 performers'. It had a civic opening in the following autumn, and continued to provide a home for both professional and amateur dramatic performances, and even early film shows, until the inscrutable workings of 'show business' enforced its closing and conversion into the garage it is today.

Though the County Hall was opened with Benson's Company in performances of plays by Tom Taylor, Shakespeare, Sheridan, Goldsmith, and Boucicault, the popular taste of the age was for spectacle, sentiment, and melodrama. The production in 1892 of *The Red Barn* is typical.

The Red Barn is a new version of a very old story which the appliances of modern times render it possible for the stage manager to produce with the most startling and also with various diverting effects. By the aid of the phantascope and limelight Mr Ellis succeeded in presenting to the audience a series of tableaux which commanded the rapt attention of the house. Commencing with a scene on Gorse Farm, in which an exceedingly intelligent donkey 'Beauty' appears, the performance passes from one striking scene to another, until an old mill, with a water-wheel in motion, is introduced. At this spot a most exciting rescue is carried out, after which the further stages of the drama are enacted in London, with the exception of an incidental visit to the Red Barn, where the murder of Mary Merton, a stage version of Maria Marten, takes place. Not only are the tragic details of this crime vividly represented, but spectral accompaniments of the most fearsome description are introduced. While the victim and her assailant are engaged in the fatal struggle, visions of Mephistopheles, the 'Death Ogre' and the gallows, serve to remind the perpetrator of the outrage of his impending punishment. For a time he escapes, and it is in the efforts to arrest the murderer that the most interesting development of the novel features of the play is witnessed. To discover the villain use is made of clairvoyance, or second sight, which a son of the murdered woman is supposed to possess. He is represented as being engaged by a detective to reproduce in a song at the Crystal Palace (an illuminated view of which was given) the various actions of the murderer when killing and disposing of his victim, and it is while this performance is proceeding that the guilt of the perpetrator of the crime is brought home to him. The excellence of the acting of Mr Lionel Ellis as the detective and the showman, and the thoroughly boy-like demeanour of Miss Bessie Ellis as the exponent of the clairvoyant art deserve especial commendation. Mr John E. Coyle as Jerry Updyke, with his intelligent donkey, the William Carlton of Mr Charles E. Wilton, the Uriah Cuthbert of Mr John Berkeley, the Mary Merton of Miss Gussie Everett, and the Betty of Miss Cossie Neel, were also very good. It is seldom that a pair are so well-matched on the stage as Jerry, the coster, and Betty, his sweetheart, were in this play. In the scenes that relieved the tragic portions of the melodrama they, with other members of the company, kept the audience in continual laughter with their humorous byplay, songs and dances.

The *Journal* also records that the production, as we might expect, proved a decided popular success, and there were full houses, except, significantly enough, in the front seats!

The nineteenth and twentieth centuries have seen a good deal of church building and restoration in the city. All three medieval parish churches have been affected—St Martin's had a large-scale restoration in 1849, the chancel of St Edmund's was completely rebuilt in 1866, and St Thomas's seems to have been worked on by every generation, being repewed twice, fitted with gas lighting, and later electricity, having a new floor,

and eventually George III's organ being transferred to it from the cathedral. The medieval 'Doom' painting over the chancel arch was uncovered, rewhitewashed, and uncovered again. It still remains to be
adequately and carefully restored.

But for the increasing population new provision was necessary, and
new parish churches were built at St Paul's Fisherton, 1853, All Saints
East Harnham, 1854, St John's Bemerton, 1860 (superseding but not
replacing George Herbert's tiny church, which was subsequently carefully restored and preserved), St Mark's, 1915, and St Francis's, 1939
(Pl. 49).

The toleration which succeeded the religious strife of earlier centuries
was marked all over the city by the springing up of churches and chapels
of various denominations. Roman Catholicism returned in 1848, with a
church in Exeter Street dedicated in honour of the founder of the first
cathedral, St Osmund (Pl. 47). The architect was A. W. Pugin. Public
opinion could still be roused against Roman Catholics, and as late as
1850 'No Popery' demonstrations were being held on the Green Croft.
But the fact that Sir John Lambert, who largely financed the building of
St Osmund's, could become Mayor of the city in 1853 exemplifies the
passing of the civil and legal restrictions which had once shackled the
members of this faith.

The last chapter has recorded how in the eighteenth century John
Wesley came to the city and preached. The nineteenth century saw a
continued expansion of the various forms of Methodism. From the
building of the chapel of the Wesleyans in St Edmund's Church Street
(1811) to that in Dews Road (1917) the city's Methodist churches provide
an interesting sequence and comment on the architectural developments
—or retrogressions—of the period.

Other religious groups, too, have left their mark on the city. The
Baptists, who as a community date from the seventeenth century, built a
lofty new chapel in Brown Street in 1829; in spite of its 650 'sittings', it
was packed to overflowing when in 1857 the great preacher and orator of
the Metropolitan Tabernacle, London, C. H. Spurgeon—then only
twenty-three—came to preach there; so popular was he that on his return
in the following year the meetings had to be held in the open air. The
new Congregational church in Fisherton Street came later, in 1879; tucked
away unobtrusively in Mill Road, the Room of the Plymouth Brethren
(1860) has no claims to architectural merit, but is part of the social
history of the period.

Most of the nonconformist communities, however stormy their experience in earlier periods, had now become accepted and respectable.
There were, however, occasional disturbances; the Salvation Army had
some unpleasant experiences in the summer of 1882 before it established
itself, and additional special constables had to be sworn in to help the
peace. Northy records that:

The assaults on the 'Army' were chiefly made by a discreditable organization with the name of the 'Skeleton Army' who were not content with throwing rotten eggs, and other filthy missiles, but who used bludgeons and other formidable weapons, and attacked defenceless females as well as men. . . . There is but little doubt that these new evangelists brought much of the trouble upon themselves by the adoption of an aggressive and uncompromising attitude, but there was nothing in their conduct to warrant the brutality and senselessness of the outrages committed against them, nor anything to excuse the indirect encouragement given to the roughs by certain prominent citizens in places of authority.

Unorthodox as some of its methods may have been, the Salvation Army brought religion to people whom the churches and chapels alike had been unable to reach, and with the realization of this the opposition to it gradually died down.

The appearance in the city of various temperance orators and the meetings of the Blue Ribbon society in the latter half of the nineteenth century reflect another social movement of the time, the attempt to combat the evils of indiscriminate drinking. A less reputable and more hysterical outburst of religious zeal inspired Mrs Girling, the leader of a curious community known as the 'Shakers', who at this time were encamped in Hampshire. On 25 November 1875 she 'lectured' at the Hamilton Hall in New Street. She had with her eight young women dressed all in white, and four men, all members of her community; her attempts to expound their religion of love were frequently interrupted both by followers and audience.

At this stage of the proceedings another young woman rose from her chair and commenced dancing with the other female, the two continuing to move round the platform in a sort of regular movement, clapping their hands, as it were, in unison. One of the girls shouted: 'Carry me home with my burden', and the other uttered various ejaculations. The audience appearing to be struck with these manifestations, expressions of astonishment were uttered, when Mrs Girling said: 'You might be quiet under the circumstances.' One of the girls then shouted, 'O glory is my spirit', and the other cried, 'O glory, we don't know where we are going.' The young women continued dancing for some time with great earnestness, occasionally singing scraps of hymns and quoting passages of scripture.

To judge from the complete contemporary press accounts a truly astonishing time was had by all.

To the student of architecture it is interesting in a city which preserves so much medieval ecclesiastical building to compare with it the nineteenth-century churches and the two examples of the contemporary approach—the new Roman Catholic church of St Gregory (1938) and the Anglican church of St Francis. Fascinating too is the study of the changed uses to which buildings have been put during the city's long history. What is now the Diocesan Church House in Crane Street, originally a very fine example of a rich merchant's house of the fifteenth century, had descended to being a workhouse before its restoration and conversion to its present use in 1881; the building in Fisherton Street which began as a Methodist chapel in 1869 has had a subsequent chequered history as cinema and repertory theatre. One of the city's historians writing in 1893 gives another example of a similar kind:

The old Temperance Hall, 62, Gigant street, having been purchased and fitted up by Mrs Sidney Lear as a Reading Room for Young Men of the Working Classes, was opened by the sub-dean, Dr Bourne. This affords an interesting example of Time's changes. In the eighteenth century it was a Quaker's Meeting House, a Quaker wedding having been solemnized there as late as 1788; there must also have been a burying ground attached, as it is recorded that in April 1772, Miss Moore, daughter of Mr James Moore, of this city, was interred in the Quakers' Burying ground at the Meeting House in Giggin-street. In the early part of the nineteenth century it became the Salisbury Infant School, probably wholly or partially rebuilt, and so it continued till the school was closed in 1878, shortly after which it was acquired by the Salisbury Temperance Society; while it is now intended to form a permanent home for the recreation of the working classes.

Rebuilt again in the eighteen-nineties, the Temperance Hall was subsequently taken over by a firm of brewers, and now forms part of their brewery.

In the public building of the time, too, significant social changes are reflected. The development of banking, the distributive trades, the vital importance in this area of agriculture, can be seen in the buildings of the banks, the department stores, and the corn exchange or Market House. (The latter, built in 1859, had for many years one of the only full-gauge private railways in the country, connecting it with the main line; part of it is still in use to supply fuel to the electricity works.) The widening and rebuilding of Fisherton Bridge in 1872 was a portent of the increasing importance, once again, of road transport; by the time of the construction of the new Harnham Bridge in 1933 that revolution was in mid career. There, now, almost side by side, stand the old and new Harnham Bridges, linking the Middle Ages with the twentieth century, an image of the city as a whole; while overhead fly the aircraft from the airfields of the Plain to remind us that with the invention of yet another form of travel another revolution is in the making.

And, dominating all, as it has done since the thirteenth century, stands the cathedral. By comparison with earlier ages, its experience during the last century and a half has been comparatively tranquil. Much in the way of repair and preservation has had to be done. Gilbert Scott had his turn in the eighteen-sixties; the steeplejacks, who rebuilt the top thirty feet of the spire and added aircraft warning lights, had theirs in 1951. In 1876 the Dean and Chapter accepted the offer of a fine new organ. Doubtless this was some consolation to Miss Chafyn Grove, whose gift it was, for the City Council's refusal five years earlier to allow her to erect an 'Early English Fountain in the Market Place'. But Wyatt's new broom in the eighteenth century had caused the last sweeping upheaval; since then the cathedral, carefully tended and loved, has settled down to a quiet and dignified middle age in its Close, which remains one of the loveliest and mose peaceful corners of contemporary England.

Cathedral and Market Place, they remain symbols of the twin forces that have moulded and shaped the city in its long history. The significance of the cathedral has often been written about; less often has that of the Market Place been noted—and yet it has both its importance and its romance. Writing at the end of the nineteenth century, W. H. Hudson saw it thus:

Business is business, and must be attended to, in fair or foul weather, but for business with pleasure we prefer it fine on market-day. The one great and chief pleasure, in which all participate, is just to be there, to be in the crowd—a joyful occasion which gives a festive look to every face. The mere sight of it exhilarates like wine. The numbers—the people and the animals! The carriers' carts drawn up in rows on rows—carriers from a hundred little villages on the Bourne, the Avon, the Wylye, the Nadder, the Ebble, and from all over the Plain, each bringing its little contingent. Hundreds and hundreds more coming by train; you see them pouring down Fisherton Street in a continuous procession, all hurrying market-wards. And what a lively scene the market presents now, full of cattle and sheep and pigs and crowds of people standing round the shouting auctioneers! And horses, too, the beribboned hacks, and ponderous draught horses with manes and tails decorated with golden straw, thundering over the stone pavement as they are trotted up and down! And what a profusion of fruit and vegetables, fish and meat, and all kinds of provisions on the stalls, where women with baskets on their arms are jostling and bargaining! The Corn Exchange is like a huge beehive, humming with the noise of talk, full of brown-faced farmers in their riding and driving clothes and leggings, standing in knots or thrusting their hands into sacks of oats or barley. You would think that all the farmers from all the Plain were congregated there. There is a joyful contagion in it all.

The detail has changed in fifty years, but not the essential spirit; and that, probably, has changed equally little since the thirteenth century.

Religion and trade, the power of both and the consequences of both, have been at the core of the city's development since the days when they brought it down from its hill and set it up again in the plain, in the 'rich champaigns and fertile valleys, abounding in the fruits of the earth, and profusely watered by living streams'. Peter of Blois was right. Seven hundred years of history, of change, of decay, of rebirth, have confirmed what he knew intuitively. Salisbury is indeed a city 'to which the whole world cannot produce a parallel'.

- -

POSTSCRIPT

CONCERNING THE CATHEDRAL

- -

THIS BOOK IS a complete historical survey in brief of the City of Salisbury. Here the reader will find, beginning with its predecessor on the hill of Old Sarum and describing all its streets and buildings as far as they are known, a history and description of one of our most important ancient towns. But there is one significant omission. Of the cathedral itself in the old city and the new, comparatively little is said. Yet Salisbury as we know it now, took its rise from the cathedral. (Frontispiece.)

It is obvious that this great building, and the services which called it into existence and gave it widespread and undying fame, could not be described here even in the barest outline, save at the cost of repeating what has already developed into something like a library, much of which is familiar to students. In writing this postscript, however, I have chosen one of the less known aspects of the story of the cathedral itself, namely, what is really meant by the 'Use of Sarum', and the far-flung influence which followed its developments. It was by this use that the name of Salisbury came to be known, far beyond the limits touched by its trade, culture, or by other means. No book about Salisbury would be complete without something of the cathedral, and nothing goes more to the heart of the matter than the special development of the services for which it was planned. So here I have said more about the cathedral and its uses and customs *outside* Salisbury than within it, and I have left the architecture, easily seen and already well described, to others who have written books solely about the cathedral.

We have to remember that the metropolitan church of Canterbury was monastic, and therefore its influence upon secular churches could never be very strong, while the second metropolitan church, that of York, could only influence a comparatively limited area. But the church of Sarum was the model great English church, a secular foundation whose services and methods could be copied anywhere. We shall see that in course of time its influence made itself felt from one end of the country to another, as well as in Scotland, Ireland, and in Wales, and even abroad.

There it still stands today, as it has done since the thirteenth century, unlike any other cathedral building because it was all produced at one time in accordance with one design; the spire, of course, being a later addition, and the only such major addition. It therefore exhibits in its plan what the men of the thirteenth century looked upon as the perfect church for all its purposes. In all the other cathedral churches there had been a gradual growth from early times, part of the fabric being conditioned by another part built long ago. Only perhaps at Exeter, and then with an important limitation of the surviving Norman towers, can we see another such medieval church, the designer of which had a perfectly free hand to build the whole thing as he wanted it, with all the fittings in the places prepared for them.

In speaking of the Church and its services the words 'Sarum Use' have constantly been employed. Now what does this mean? It might in these circumstances be said that it includes the building with all its perfection in architecture and design, but the phrase is more properly used of the services, the way they were carried out, and the constitution of the great body of clergy whose lot it was to make the necessary provision day in and day out for the orderly working of the establishment. Let us now try to see clearly something of the nature of these services.

In the earlier centuries after the Peace of the Church, forms of service developed differently in different areas. In Western Christendom after the break up of the Roman Empire, in what is now France and Spain, there was a great variety of liturgies called Gallican. Charles the Great in the eighth century set himself to remedy this, since he wanted uniformity throughout his dominions. He sent to Rome for copies of the Roman books. Then he and his scholars set about framing a new liturgy for general use. They took the Roman outline and filled it in with Gallican matter, or rather with selections from it. The liturgy so revised was actually accepted in Rome itself and became the Roman rite of later days, but the non-Roman matter was variable, and particularly in the use of the scripture parts; it varied from place to place. The framework and the Canon of the Mass or Prayer of Consecration were fixed, but there was room for considerable variety in other things. The rite of Salisbury was one among these rites, Roman in the main, in contrast with what went before, Gallican in the subsidiary parts. Such rites came to us with the Normans: in earlier times we have evidence to show that the Saxons were trying to follow the Roman rite. This presumably is what existed before the alterations under Charles the Great.

In considering the question of these large churches which were in the hands of an elaborate organization, either the cathedral Chapter or a monastic one, we have to remember that alongside the services and the rules for carrying them out there were the rules for the working of the establishment, the duties and the privileges of the various officials. The cathedral Chapter of secular canons lived round the church: they owned property and were not under monastic vows, but they were bound to carry out all the services of the Church in the best and most perfect manner, and behind it all there was the question of finance. There were usually four principal canons, the Dean, Precentor, Chancellor, and Treasurer, besides other canons and clergy of minor rank. At Salisbury and those cathedrals influenced by the Sarum establishment, the Dean was the head of the Chapter, the Precentor had the responsibility of the choir and the music, the Chancellor had the responsibility of the schools and the legal and secretarial concerns of the whole body, while the Treasurer had to do with the plate, vestments, and valuables of all kinds. Some Chapters were not constituted like this, but their officials bore different names and their duties were generally spread among them.

A word should be added to explain what is meant by a church of the Old Foundation and that of a new one. This does not refer to medieval varieties of organization but to the distinction between a Chapter of the old traditional type and one set up to take the place of a monastic Chapter after the suppression of the monasteries. Thus, while Salisbury is a church of the Old Foundation, Winchester is one of the New. We are not concerned with a new foundation.

The site at Old Sarum was fortified from earliest times, undoubtedly pre-Roman, and the date of the building of the first Christian church there is unknown. But the first cathedral was built by St Osmund and completed in 1092, being severely damaged soon after. It was either rebuilt or extensively repaired by Bishop Roger, probably within a year or two of his appointment to the see.

This Norman cathedral of Old Sarum was not a very large building. However, it was big enough to make provision for the services to be carried out with the greatest dignity and splendour, although we must not think of it as being of the very large type, such as we see at Norwich and Peterborough. For example, it was not nearly as big as Exeter, but the services reached their full development while this building was still in use, and the famous Sarum books of Services and Directions were being already carried out in this cathedral church before being moved down to New Sarum to the church begun there in 1220.

We now recall the policy of the Normans with regard to cathedrals. The cathedrals of Saxon times were small buildings in small places, and the Normans wished to have bigger cathedrals in important centres, so the Saxon cathedrals of Ramsbury and Sherborne gave place to the new Norman one built at Old Sarum. In two other instances, the important new Norman churches of Lincoln and York, the arrangement worked well enough, but at Sarum the canons complained of interference from the military in the nearby castle, and not being able to get enough water on the desolate chalk hill. So in 1217 it was determined to abandon the old cathedral and build a really splendid new one in the valley near by where so many rivers meet. This meant that the building could be developed without any restrictions (Pls. 36, 46). We must not forget that the magnificent thirteenth-century church which we now see is probably the most perfect building of its time. Lincoln may have richer detail, and we may have to turn to individual churches for special features, but taking the building as an architectural whole there is nothing so complete and perfect as Salisbury. What afterwards became the traditional English eastern termination to a cathedral church, namely the square end with a chapel east of the high altar, whose vault is on a lower level than that of the choir, may be very largely due to Salisbury's influence. We recall the way in which the east ends of this kind cover the country from Chichester and St Albans to Chester, while in the eastern counties we have the full height of the choir carried to the east end of the building in the manner so familiar at York and Carlisle.[1]

An interesting point often overlooked is the similarity between the fourteenth-century detail of the central tower of Hereford and that in a like position at Salisbury.

We are particularly fortunate in the books which have survived from the medieval church at Salisbury. There are the Foundation Documents of St Osmund, largely constitutional, there are the Consuetudinary and *Ordinale* giving the fullest directions for the carrying out of the services and other matter of the kind, besides the service books giving the text of the Rite, which of course were necessary for any church, such as the Missal, the Breviary, and the Processional. When we hear of some church being constituted in medieval times on the model of Salisbury, this may refer to the establishment alone or it may also refer to the text of the services and the ceremonial accompanying it. This is why we find that in some places the Salisbury text of the services was in use, but not the exact ceremonial used in Salisbury Cathedral. It was the constitutional books which had so much influence outside. As early as the later part of the twelfth century the Dean and Chapter of Glasgow sent for the books for their guidance, as they wanted to follow the use of Sarum, the church of St Andrews in Scotland being again, like Canterbury, no model for a secular church, as the Chapter was one of Augustinian Canons. If we recall the political history of the time we shall see how unlikely it was that the Chapters of Scotland would turn to York for anything. As a matter of fact, the diocese of Moray did turn to Lincoln, but not until after Lincoln had itself adopted a certain amount of matter from Sarum, and the next thing we find is that in 1242 the Dean and Chapter of Moray decided to adopt the Use of Sarum in everything in Elgin cathedral.

There is evidence that other Scottish cathedrals, including Dunkeld and of course Aberdeen, were influenced by Sarum, and as far as liturgical books and fragments go every one that has survived from the medieval Church of Scotland is a book of Sarum Use, except of course those written for the houses of religious orders which had their own Uses. Apparently the decision of the Synod of Cashel in Ireland in 1172 to

---

[1] The last east end built in the Salisbury manner is that of the late fifteenth-century Gothic Collegiate Church of Roslin in Scotland.

follow what was done in England seems to have carried with it, in some places at any rate, the following of Sarum Use. Henry of London, Archbishop of Dublin, brought Sarum books into the cathedrals there early in the next century. In fact one of the best surviving manuscripts of the Sarum Consuetudinary is one that belonged to Dublin. It would be dangerous, however, to assume that these English books were followed all over Ireland.

Coming back to England, we find again and again the influence of Sarum. There were other notable secular cathedrals which had their own Use, Hereford, for example, but the area in which it was used was comparatively small. We find many traces of other great churches having had their own liturgical Use, yet in two instances at least giving way to the Use of Sarum. We might make a list of these definite prescriptions of Sarum Use: St George, Windsor, 1352; St Mary's College, St David's, 1372; King's College, Cambridge, and All Souls, Oxford, 1443; Eton, 1444; Battlesfield, Salop, 1445. Some of the religious houses followed Sarum Use, e.g. Augustinian Canons at Barnwell near Cambridge and Minoresses at Bruisyard in Suffolk, 1376.

The old Use of London gave way to Sarum early in 1415, and some- thing of the same kind happened at Lichfield about 1420. In the founda- tion of the collegiate church of Chester-le-Street near Durham the Archbishop of York prescribed either the Use of York or that of Sarum in 1268; and in 1542 Convocation adopted the Use of Sarum for the Breviary Services all over the Southern Province. Indeed, we believe that Lincoln Use, mentioned as it is in the Preface to the Prayer Book, was by that time little more than a name, and almost identical with the Sarum. This had become so much the case that if we find a book which purports to be 'According to the Use of England' we shall always find that that book is really according to the Use of Sarum. One particular instance may be quoted. When that wise and statesmanlike Bishop of Exeter, John Grandisson, who completed the building of that cathedral, was appointed, it was immediately after the mob in London had stolen the belongings of his predecessor, Bishop Stapeldon, and the new Bishop arrived from Avignon with apparently only the Roman Pontifical. Now the English Order for blessing the holy oils differs in some respects from the Roman. So the first thing that the Bishop did was to write to the Archdeacon of Sarum to see if he could provide him with a Book of English Use. We have Grandisson's correspondence with Pope John XXII in which the Bishop refers to his having been enthroned in Exeter Cathedral 'according to the English Use without any fuss'. This is a good example of the respect and the weight that the Use of Sarum carried in medieval times.

At the end of the fifteenth century the Sarum Books used in Scotland had become confused with manuscript additions containing services for local saints' days, of which there were many, added without regard to the main part of the book. The situation was rather like that in Exeter in the fourteenth century. Towards the end of the century the great Bishop of Aberdeen, William Elphinstone, the founder of the university, took the matter of the Breviary in hand, and he reconstructed it and printed a revision in 1509–10 which claimed to be for the whole kingdom of Scotland, in place of Sarum books. This was really a careful reform of the Sarum Breviary to provide properly for the large number of local saints, and did not go farther afield on the lines of the Continental Breviary reforms of the period. King James IV and his Council gave an Edinburgh printer a monopoly of printing and sale, describing it as 'our own Scots Use' and forbidding the sale of Sarum books. But it was not very long before the printers complained that others were infringing their rights by printing Sarum books. Alas, we know no more of the story, and the Aberdeen Breviary is only a small book, obviously for private use and not suitable for services in choir. But the fact remains that the Sarum Rite underwent this very important revision and was intended to be adopted as the national Use of the whole country. There are other cases where the Sarum Rite was followed outside England, but these were in private chapels.

We may note that the idea of one Rite serving the whole country and not merely one or two dioceses occurs in its most striking form in Scotland. In 1519 Eric Walkendorf, Archbishop of Trondhjem, printed a missal which he claimed to be for the whole kingdom of Norway.

We have traced the Sarum Use, liturgical, constitutional, and architectural, from unknown sources in Normandy to a sort of concentration here at Salisbury, and then all over the country and beyond it. We have seen its adoption in Scotland and the attempt to turn it into the national Use there. Last of all, we have to remember that so far as the present Prayer Book derives from one of the Latin Rites, it is from Sarum and not from the others that it comes. For example, like the Sarum Missal, we have Sundays after Trinity: and the Gospels for Advent Sunday and the second Sunday in Advent are those from the Sarum Rite, and this is also the case with both Epistle and Gospel on Trinity Sunday. Even within the last century those responsible for reviving the old Ceremonial, in spite of considerable lack of knowledge, turned to the Sarum books and not to the Roman (or what they thought was the Roman practice, which is a comparatively recent aberration, fortunately not as yet very widespread in England).

There has grown up in modern times a false and misleading use of the word Sarum. It has been used to indicate not only things belonging to or characteristic of the Use of Sarum, but also things in no way peculiar to Salisbury. A Sarum altar is spoken of, meaning the normal type of altar, no doubt used at Salisbury, but not exclusively there. The word has also been used of a chasuble with a Yshaped orphrey such as might be found almost anywhere of old. The word Sarum has been used of a particular

L

shade of red. This is wholly because some people in the nineteenth century, reading the Sarum colour rubric, thought so many days were kept in red that there must have been a subdued shade of it for ferial days, so they invented a special Sarum red which never existed.

This book has been largely concerned with material things, either buildings or manufactures which in medieval and modern times the people of Salisbury have distributed to the country and the Continent. These last few pages, while covering no new ground, bring together what was scattered in many books, and explain what is meant by the Sarum Use, that intangible commodity which Sarum Old and New has distributed through the centuries to an even wider field.

BIBLIOGRAPHIES

CHAPTER I

Antiquaries Journal, xv (1935), 174–92: 'Trial Excavations in the East Suburb of Old Sarum', J. F. S. Stone and John Charlton

Archaeological Journal, civ (1948), 129–43: 'Old Sarum', D. H. Montgomerie, with two notes by Sir Alfred Clapham

GOVER, J. E. B., MAWER, Allen, and STENTON, F. M., *The Place-Names of Wiltshire*, 1939

INGRAM, James (trans.), *The Anglo-Saxon Chronicle*, 1923

JONES, W. H., *Domesday for Wiltshire*, Bath, 1865

—, *The Register of St Osmund*, 2 vols. (Rolls series, 1883–4), especially the introduction to vol. ii

PRICE, Francis, *A Description of the Cathedral Church of Salisbury*, appendix, 'An Account of Old Sarum, etc.', Salisbury, 1787

Proceedings of the Society of Antiquaries of London, 2nd series, xxii (1911), 190–200, 501–18; xxiv (1912), 52–65; xxv (1913), 93–104; xxvi (1914), 100–19; xxvii (1915), 230–8; xxviii (1916), 174–84: reports on the excavations, Sir William Hope and Lt-Col. W. Hawley

REED, T. D., *The Battle for Britain in the Fifth Century*, 1944

STOKES, Ethel, *Wiltshire Inquisitiones post Mortem, Edward III*, 1914, 16

Victoria County History of Wiltshire, ii (Anglo-Saxon period and Domesday), 1955

WANSEY, Henry, *A Plan of Old Sarum with its History and References*, Salisbury, 1819

Wiltshire Archaeological Magazine, i (1854), 132–95, 'Leland's Journey through Wiltshire', J. E. Jackson; x (1867), 253–322, 'Ancient Chapels, etc., in Co. Wilts.', J. E. Jackson; liii (1950), 153–83, 'Salisbury Cathedral Manuscripts', Neil R. Ker; lvi (1955), 55–9, 'The Choir of Old Sarum Cathedral', Hugh Braun, and 102–26, 'Sorviodunum', J. F. S. Stone and D. J. Algar

CHAPTER II

ECCLESTON, Thomas of, *Monumenta Franciscana*, Rolls series, 1858

FLETCHER, J. M. J., *Bishop Giles de Bridport and De Vaux College*, 1934; reprinted from the *Wiltshire Gazette*

HASKINS, C., *Salisbury Charters and the History of St Edmund's College*, 1927

Journal of the British Archaeological Association, 3rd series, iv (1939), 55–115, 'The Houses of Salisbury Close in the Fourteenth Century', Kathleen Edwards

Oxoniensia, xix (1954), 61–91, 'The Activities of Some Fellows of De Vaux College, Salisbury, at Oxford and Elsewhere', Kathleen Edwards

TREVELYAN, G. M., *English Social History*, 1942, chapters 1–4

Wiltshire Archaeological Magazine, xxxix (1917), 'The Relations of the Bishops and Citizens of Salisbury between 1225 and 1612', Fanny Street; xlvii (1937), 36–54, 'Grey Friars of Salisbury', A. G. Little; xlix (1942), 435–79, 'Notes on the History of the Church House', C. R. Everett

WORDSWORTH, C., *St Nicholas Hospital, Salisbury*, 1903

— and MACLEANE, D., *Statutes of Salisbury Cathedral*, 1915

CHAPTER III

ANONYMOUS, *A Discoverie of Six Women Preachers*, 1641

BRAY, William (ed.), *Diary of John Evelyn*, 1895; entry under 20 July 1654

BROWN, Ivor, *Shakespeare*, 1949, 262

FEA, Allan, *The Flight of the King*, 2nd edn 1908

FLETCHER, J. M. J., *The Gorges Monument in Salisbury Cathedral*; reprinted from the *Wiltshire Gazette*, 1932

—, *The Hertford Monument in Salisbury Cathedral*; reprinted from the *Wiltshire Gazette*, 1932

FOXE, John, *Book of Martyrs*, iii, 1631, 679, Maundrel

FULLER, Thomas, *The History of the Worthies of England*, ii, 1811, 440, Maundrel and Coberly

Historical Manuscripts Commission, iv, City of Salisbury (1907), 191–254

IVIE, John, *Declaration*, 1661

JONES, W. H., *Diocesan Histories, Salisbury*, 1880

WALTON, Izaak, *The Works of George Herbert in Prose and Verse*, n.d., containing 'The Life of Mr George Herbert'

Wiltshire Archaeological Magazine, xiii (1872), 119–88, 252–73; xiv (1874), 38–67; xv (1875), 1–41, 235, on Penruddock; xxviii (1896), 315; xxx (1899), 20–34, on the fall of Wiltshire monasteries; xxix (1897), 159–61, on witchcraft; xlvii (1937), 379–405, 'Notes on the Prebendal Mansion of Sherborne Monastery', C. R. Everett

Wiltshire County Records, iv (1949), Recusancy

Wiltshire Notes and Queries, i (1896), 183–8, on Henry Sherfield; v (1908), 433–42, on Wilton House

CHAPTER IV

AUBREY, John, *Brief Lives*, ed. Anthony Powell, 1949

BURNET, Gilbert, Bishop of Salisbury, *The History of His own Times*, 1823

DODSWORTH, William, *An Historical Account of the Episcopal See and Cathedral Church of Sarum*, 1814, pt i, chapter 3; pt iii, chapter 4

FELLOWES, E. H., *English Cathedral Music*, 1948, 148–50; Michael Wise

FLETCHER, J. M. J., *Notes on Salisbury Cathedral*, Salisbury, 1924

FLETCHER, J. M. J., *Some Royal Visits to the City and Cathedral Church of the Blessed Virgin Mary at Salisbury*, Salisbury, 1935

Friends of Salisbury Cathedral, *20th Annual Report*, 1950, 'Wyatt's "Improvements"', Sir Bruce Richmond

HEAPE, R. Grundy, *Salisbury; Some Architecture in the City and the Close*, 1934

H.M.S.O., *Report of the Royal Commission on Charities*, 1906

MORRIS, Christopher (ed.), *The Journeys of Celia Fiennes*, 1949

OLIVIER, Edith, *Wiltshire* (1951), 267–70; Sir Stephen Fox

POPE, Walter, *The Life of the Right Reverend Father in God, Seth, Lord Bishop of Salisbury*, 1697

POWELL, Anthony, *John Aubrey and His Friends*, 1948

WHEATLEY, H. B. (ed.), *Diary of Samuel Pepys* (1923), v. 27, 41, 89; viii. 39, 40

Wiltshire Archaeological Magazine, l (1944), 425–45, 'Notes on the Decanal and other Houses in the Close of Sarum', C. R. Everett

CHAPTER V

CHILD, Miss, *The Spinster at Home in the Close of Salisbury*, 1844

COBBETT, William, *Rural Rides*, 1802–35

DOUGLAS, M. A., and ASH, C. R., *The Godolphin School*, 1928

GODDARD, E. H., *Wiltshire Bibliography*, 1929

HAPPOLD, F. C. (comp.), *Bishop Wordsworth's School, 1890–1950*, 1950

HASKINS, Charles, *The History of Salisbury Infirmary*, 1922

HUDSON, W. H., *A Shepherd's Life on Salisbury Plain*, 1910

'J. B.', *The Salisbury Guide*, 1848

Motor, The, 4 June 1952, 'The Scout Car', Patrick Macnaghten

Salisbury Journal, The, from 1790

Salisbury Times, The, from 1868

SHARP, Thomas, *Newer Sarum*, 1949

STEVENS, Frank, *The Salisbury Museums, 1861–1947*, 1947

TOYNBEE, William (ed.), *The Diaries of William Charles Macready, 1833–1900*, 1912

TROLLOPE, Anthony, *Autobiography*, 1883

Views and Reviews, special edition, Salisbury, 1897

WHEELER, W. A., *Supplemental Sarum Chronology, 1881–1900*, 1901

POSTSCRIPT

Archaeologia, lxviii (1917), 43–110, 'Quire Screens in English Churches'; 111–26, 'The Sarum Consuetudinary and its Relation to the Cathedral Church of Old Sarum', both by Sir William St John Hope

COOK, G. H., *Portrait of Salisbury Cathedral*, 1949

DAYMAN, E. A., and JONES, W. H. R., *Statutes of the Cathedral Church of Sarum*, Bath, 1883

DICKINSON, H. F., *The Sarum Missal*, 1861–83

EDWARDS, Kathleen, *The English Secular Cathedrals in the Middle Ages*, 1949

FRERE, Walter W. H., *The Use of Sarum*, 1898

PROCTOR, F., and WORDSWORTH, C., *The Sarum Breviary*, 1882–6

THOMPSON, A. Hamilton, *The Cathedral Churches of England*, 1925

WORDSWORTH, C., *Sarum Processions and Ceremonies*, 1901

GENERAL BIBLIOGRAPHY

BENSON, Robert, and HATCHER, Henry, *Old and New Sarum or Salisbury*, 1843

CASSAN, S. H., *Lives and Memoirs of the Bishops of Sherborne and Salisbury*, Salisbury, 1824

DORLING, E. E., *History of Salisbury*, 1911

HALL, P., *Picturesque Memorials of Salisbury*, 1834

HASKINS, C., *The Ancient Trade Guilds and Companies of Salisbury*, 1912

JONES, W. H. R., *Fasti Ecclesiae Sarisberiensis*, Salisbury, 1879

JOWITT, R. L. P., *Salisbury*, 1951

LEDWICH, Edward, *Antiquitates Sarisburienses*, Salisbury, 1771

NORTHY, T. J., *The Popular History of Old and New Sarum*, 1897

NOYES, E., *Salisbury Plain*, 1913

ROBERTSON, Dora H., *Sarum Close*, 1938

STEVENS, F. (ed.), *The Festival Book of Salisbury*, 1914

Victoria History of Wiltshire, iii (ecclesiastical), 1956

WHEELER, W. A., *Sarum Chronology*, 1889

INDEX